W9-CNA-258

OVER INDONESIA

PHOTOGRAPHY BY RIO HELMI & GUIDO ALBERTO ROSSI / TEXT BY MICHAEL VATIKIOTIS

ADDITIONAL PHOTOGRAPHY BY DIANE GRAHAM GARTH, GEORG GERSTER, LEONARD LUERAS, KAL MULLER AND LUCA INVERNIZZI TETTONI

ARCHIPELAGO PRESS

CONTENTS

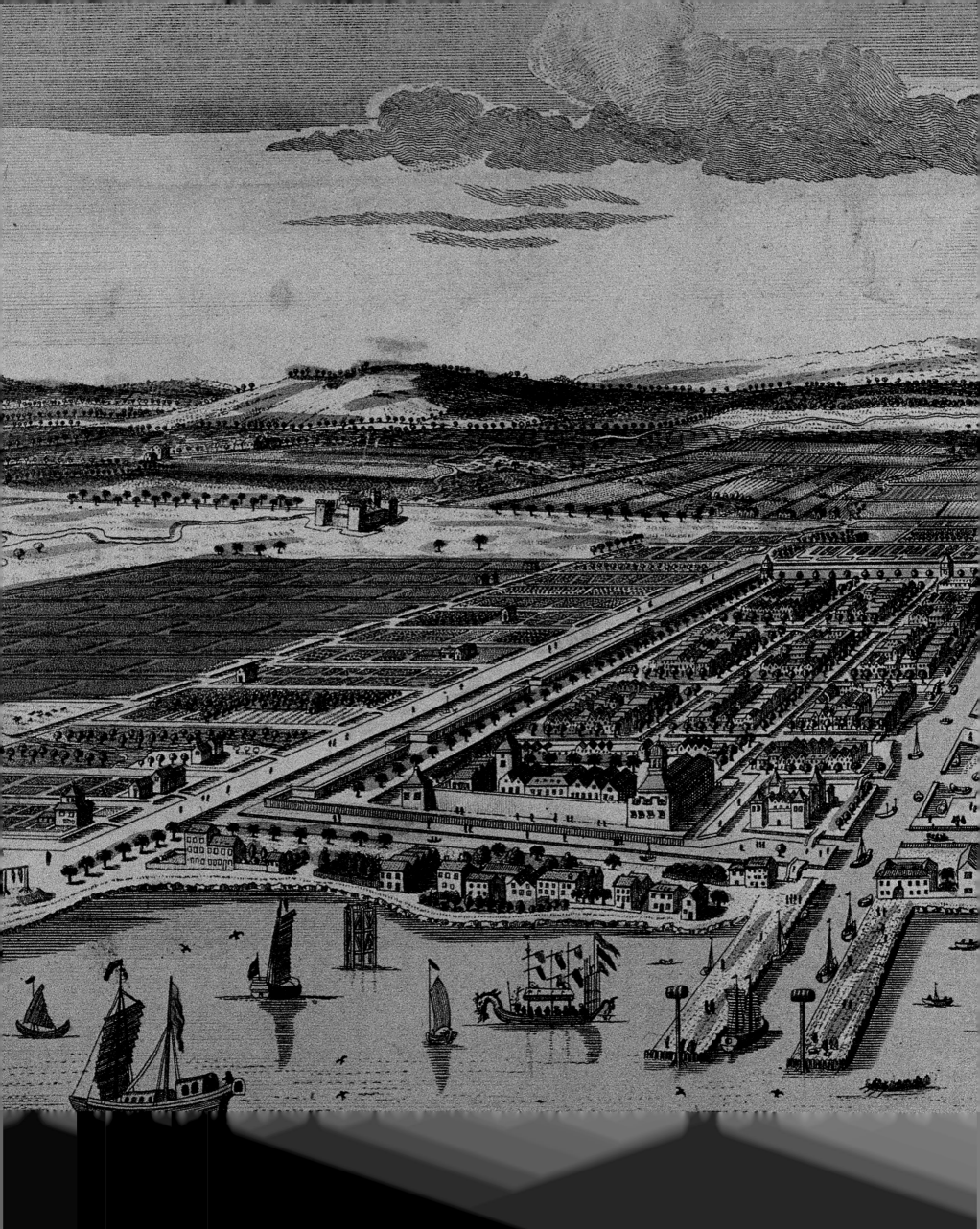

UNDER THE RAINBOW

Views of the Javanese countryside. Top, Gunung Sumbung. The lithograph is by C.W. Meiling after F. Junghuhn, 1864. Junghuhn, a German doctor, was also a keen observer and explorer of the Javanese landscape. His enthusiasm often led him into danger—expeditions to the summits of Java's volcanoes were not easy in those days, and exposure to bad weather and poisonous gases were among the commonest of hazards. Bottom, this plate by the Dutch artist F.C. Wilsen was first published in 1865 in a collection entitled The Indian Archipelago: Scenes Drawn from the Nature and Life of the People. The collection featured the work of several famous artists, including the Indonesian painter Raden Saleh.

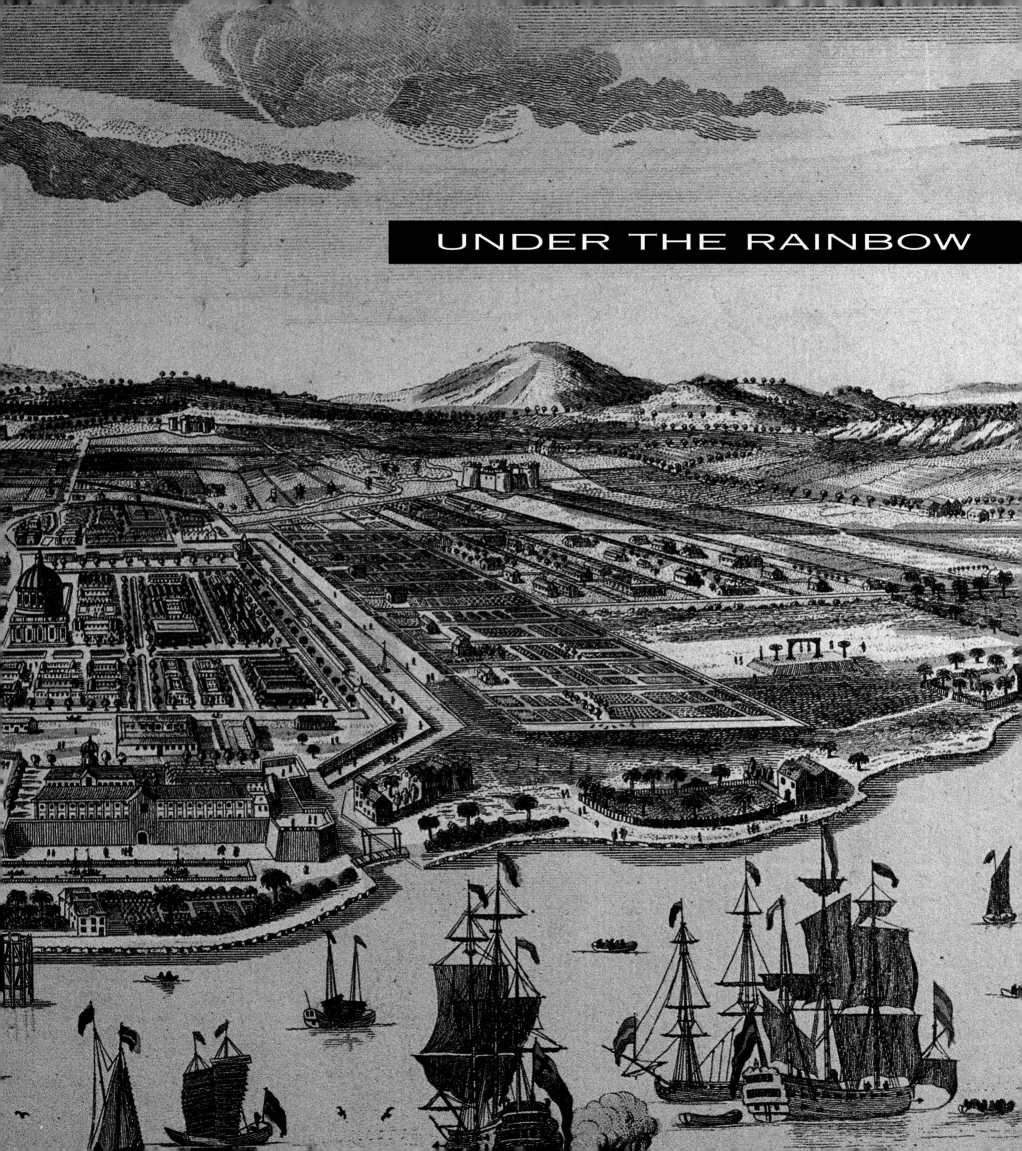

Viewing Indonesia from above is possibly the only way to comprehend the size and diversity of this complex patchwork of landscapes and cultures. On the ground it is easy to underestimate dimensions or even miss key features altogether—geographical features seem to alter every few hundred yards; there is virtually no uniformity to the landscape. This variety is mirrored in a society as diverse as the land it inhabits, a colourful profusion of cultures and customs existing in rhythmic harmony. Aptly, the Indonesian writer Mochtar Lubis calls his country 'The Land Under the Rainbow.'

Consisting of over thirteen thousand islands strung in a rough arc between the Indian and Pacific oceans and spanning a distance greater than the width of North America, Indonesia is vast enough to make the term 'archipelago' seem almost an understatement. At school, Indonesian children are taught the phrase 'from Sabang to Merauke'. These are the names of places at the two extremities of the nation. Sabang, an island off the coast of Aceh at the northwestern tip of Sumatra, was an important coaling station in the days of the steamship. Merauke is a dusty town set in the swamps of lowland Irian Jaya, some eight thousand kilometres to the south and east. Neither place is remotely like the other, situated as they are in different climatic, natural and even cultural environments.

Such diversity is the essence of Indonesia. In the nineteenth century the writer and naturalist Alfred Wallace described the archipelago as 'comparable with the divisions of the globe.' In the course of his Indonesian travels, Wallace collected vocabularies from almost sixty distinct languages. The actual number spoken is far greater.

Yet long before the arrival of Europeans in the region, travel and its companion trade had already established links between the peoples of the archipelago, and a common medium of communication existed in the Malay language. Portuguese Jesuit missionaries arriving in the Moluccas in the sixteenth century found that Malay had become, in the words of chronicler Antonio Galvao, 'like Latin in Europe.' Seaborne trade was an excellent conductor of culture and religion, bearing not only the Malay language but the teachings of Prophet Mohammed.

Trade fared rather more poorly as a conductor of hegemony. In the thirteenth century, the great Mongol emperor of China, Kublai Khan, attempted to impose his authority on the kingdoms of Java. The Javanese sent his emissary back to Peking with his ears cut off. The insulted emperor dispatched a punitive force in 1293. It was routed. Even the Europeans—first the Portuguese, then the Dutch—with their superior military and administrative skills, found it nearly impossible to overpower all

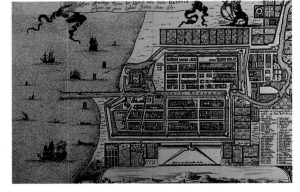

A 1754 view of old Batavia, preceding pages, conveys a perhaps exaggerated sense of order and Dutch colonial pride. The map of the city, left, was made during the tenure of Jan Pieterszoon Coen, Batavia's founder and first governor-general. Coen, a former accountant, was more or less single-handedly responsible for the establishment of Dutch power in Java.

These very rare views of Makasar, top, and Aceh, bottom, made in the middle of the seventeenth century, are from the secret files of the Dutch East India Company. They remained hidden from the eyes of the world until 1981, when a facsimile edition of 1,000 copies was circulated among antiquarians and specialists.

DE STADT SAMBOPPE INTRYCK MACASSER.

Atchyn

Views of the Javanese countryside. Top, Gunung Sumbung. The lithograph is by C.W. Meiling after F. Junghuhn, 1864. Junghuhn, a German doctor, was also a keen observer and explorer of the Javanese landscape. His enthusiasm often led him into danger— expeditions to the summits of Java's volcanoes were not easy in those days, and exposure to bad weather and poisonous gases were among the commonest of hazards. Bottom, this plate by the Dutch artist F.C. Wilsen was first published in 1865 in a collection entitled The Indian Archipelago: Scenes Drawn from the Nature and Life of the People. The collection featured the work of several famous artists, including the Indonesian painter Raden Saleh.

these islands. But neither were they entirely unsuccessful, since rival states and rulers could never bury their differences long enough to resist colonial rule effectively. The next three hundred and fifty years were marked by incessant revolt and warfare.

Puri Kehen, Bangli, south Bali. This picture by an unknown photographer was originally published in 1925.

The Dutch arrived in Java at the end of the sixteenth century. At the dawn of the twentieth, they had yet to subdue the entire archipelago—colonial forces were still fighting for control of Aceh. The Aceh wars were among the longest and bloodiest fought by any European power in the region. In fact, Dutch rule extended fully over what was known then as the Dutch East Indies for only a comparatively brief portion of their long history in the archipelago. Almost as soon as the Acehnese were placated, the first nationalist movement was established—by Javanese intellectuals, in 1908.

Indonesia's nationalist struggle is the fulcrum of the country's modern identity. Today's Indonesians are intensely proud of the manner in which they threw off the colonial yoke, styling it a 'revolution', and glorifying its leaders. Indonesian nationalism first took root among the upper classes, whom the Dutch had chosen to educate as part of a strategy to alienate the aristocracy from their people. Given the very European liberal notions these Indonesians absorbed along with their education, however, it was inevitable that such a strategy would backfire. A concerned elite began to examine the harsh, exploitative system wherewith the Dutch wrung land and labour from their people.

The Japanese occupation of the Dutch East Indies in 1942 accelerated the emancipation process, offering newly-awakened Indonesian intellectuals a chance to seize freedom on behalf of their people. Independence from Holland was declared on 17 August 1945, while the country was still under the rule of the Japanese.

As the victorious Allies swept across Southeast Asia, the Dutch attempted to regain possession of their colony. A hastily-raised nationalist army, consisting of a hodge-podge of semi-autonomous gangs and Japanese-trained militia, struggled to unite the fledgling nation against its former masters. Squabbling factions within the new republican government and attempts by Communists to seize power ensured that the struggle involved as much infighting as it did resistance against the Dutch, who labelled their attempts to regain control a simple 'police action'.

The Indonesian army, led by General Sudirman, employed guerrilla tactics to deprive the Dutch of a foothold in the Javanese heartland. In the end, international opinion favoured the emergent republic, and the Dutch were forced to negotiate. A United States of Indonesia was mooted, and rejected. Ultimately, a unitary Republic of Indonesia was established after 1949, led by the man who had declared independence in the first place: Sukarno.

Colonial life in the Dutch East Indies at the turn of the century. Top, a wreath-laying ceremony at the foot of the Celebes monument at Makasar on the eve of the birthday of the Queen of the Netherlands; this sort of ceremony took place annually at all war memorials in the East Indies. Bottom, afternoons of leisure. Europeans in starched whites taking their stroll during the cooler part of the day. Medan, Sumatra, c. 1905.

Kali Mas, Surabaya, around 1915, seen from the observation tower. The hand-tinted photograph was originally published as a postcard. The name of the photographer remains unknown to this day.

Though rich in resources, Sukarno's Indonesia was desperately poor and underdeveloped, its people accustomed to eking out a meagre existence. Their basic needs required urgent attention, but Sukarno was keen to erect the brash symbols of modern nationhood. He commissioned Jakarta's first tall buildings: a modern hotel and the thrusting independence monument in Merdeka Square. These grand designs barely masked the poverty and despair lurking in the side streets and poor urban neighbourhoods. Soon the first stirrings of discontent were felt. Sukarno urged his people to maintain the revolutionary spirit which won them their freedom. He made 'politics the commander', a policy which did little to foster stability in the country. Indonesia in the 1950s and early 1960s became a hotbed of radicalism and ferment, home to the largest Communist party in the world outside China.

Turmoil gave way to a new era of order and development under Indonesia's second president, Suharto. Suharto's New Order government turned its back on the politicization of the masses and concentrated instead on economic development, harnessing the country's immense mineral wealth—notably oil and gas—and achieving self-sufficiency in rice, the staple food. Under Suharto, Indonesia has transformed itself from one of the world's poorest countries, burdened by a lack of development and a rapidly increasing population, into an incipient Southeast Asian economic miracle. Foreign investment has poured in, attracted by cheap and plentiful labour and liberal economic policies. The government has made strenuous efforts to extend the fruits of development to the most remote corners of the Republic. Almost the entire population now has access to at least a primary education, and nearly every rural villager has access to a clinic. A successful family-planning programme has contained the population explosion, though the current population of 180 million is still likely to exceed 200 million by the turn of the century.

Yet for all this change and progress, the view from above retains a basic contrast innate to the archipelago, of land shaped by man and land untouched and even untouchable by humanity. An aerial journey through Indonesia often begins with a flight across the island of Java, a landscape so moulded by centuries of settlement that the resulting forms appear to be natural. A hop across from the eastern tip of Java lies the island of Bali. Inscriptions show that Balinese kingdoms existed in the eighth century A.D. and that the ancient Balinese kings commissioned massive irrigation works which changed the face of their island forever. Though they appear natural, Bali's contour-hugging terraced ricefields and dreamy coconut groves are a testament to man's power to shape a landscape.

At the other extreme are parts of Sumatra and great tracts of Kalimantan (on the island of Borneo) where it is hard to detect any trace of settlement at all; the seemingly endless carpet of forest, punctuated by a brownish ribbon of a river or a plunging waterfall, is all there is to be seen. Here, scattered tribes of forest-dwellers continue to live much as they always have. Some have only been introduced to the twentieth century within the past few decades.

Approaching any town in Indonesia by air, one sees much the same sort of view: a patchwork of rice fields and gardens shaded by coconut groves which soon gives way to a mosaic of rusted-tin or red-tiled rooftops. Indonesian towns share similar characteristics on the ground as well: the market area with its cluttered rows of shophouses, the administrative centre and its clusters of government buildings, the hawkers and foodstalls offering the ubiquitous sate or spicy Minangkabau food from West Sumatra, the mosques and churches, the Chinese medicine shops, barber shops and modest provincial hotels—common sights from Sabang to Merauke, as the saying goes.

Indonesia is urbanizing at a terrific rate. The capital city, Jakarta, is home to over seven million people, with many more flooding into the city from its expansive outskirts to work during the day. Surabaya in East Java, Bandung in West Java and Medan in North Sumatra all have populations in excess of two million. In most of these cities, incessant construction of modern office and shopping complexes push densely-packed urban villages to the fringes.

Indonesian cities bear all the hallmarks of progress and change, while its rural areas remain traditional and tranquil. It is here that Indonesia's spiritual strength dwells, in the ageless myths and rituals of the people. In the rural Islamic schools of Java, in Balinese Hindu temples marooned among the ricefields, in the simple tin-roofed churches of Ambon in the Moluccas and in the minds of Indonesians everywhere, the influence of religion weighs deeply.

The mystical substratum is also strong. Shapes and forms in the landscape are associated with myths and legends of the distant animistic past. The syncretism and tolerance which is a hallmark of Indonesian society fosters

Batavia was demolished at the beginning of the nineteenth century, not by war or earthquake but at the order of Governor-General Willem Daendls, who used the bricks and stones thus obtained to rebuild the city in grand style. Spacious, tree-lined avenues lined with buildings in Neoclassical style marked Daendls's refurbished city—a far cry from the bustling, crowded Jakarta of today.

their survival and may even, in a sense, originate from them. The angry sea which crashes on the southern coast of Java is home to Nyai Roro Kidul, Goddess of the Southern Sea. In her mythic, eternal union with the Sultans of the Central Javanese Kingdom of Mataram, Nyai Roro Kidul is the perfect example of the nexus between the supernatural and reality which colours Javanese society. The supernatural is a forbidding world of spirits and ogres, complex and inexplicable, while reality is life itself—a simple existence in harmony with nature, ruled by fate.

These pictures are reproductions from an album presented by the officers of the Army of the Dutch East Indies to her Majesty the Queen and His Royal Highness the Prince of the Netherlands on 7 February, 1926. Top, army aeroplanes fly above government buildings, Bandung. Bottom, the crater of a volcano near Kadiri, photographed from above.

ABOVE: THE IDJEN PLATEAU

MIDDLE: MOUNTAIN
LANDSCAPE IN
THE PREANGER

RAILWAY BRIDGE IN THE PREANGER

The text reads like advertising copy, but this is actually a page from a book entitled The Importance of Java Seen From The Air, edited and compiled by one H.M. De Vries with the cooperation of the Military Air Force, the State Railways and the Municipalities. Then, as now, Java's magnificent scenery was one of its prime attractions, though a true representation of the island's beauty was impossible before the perfection of colour photography.

TOURISM IN JAVA

Now that we have regarded Java from a commercial standpoint let us turn our thoughts to its qualities as a tourist resort. Without running the risk of being accused of exaggeration it may safely be said that there are very few countries in the world which can offer the tourist such a variety of attractions under such excellent climatic conditions. People who have never visited Java are apt to jump to the conclusion that being near the equator it must be unbearably hot; this is, however, not the case. Certainly it is summer all the year round, but it is only really hot in the coast towns during the changing of the monsoons and even then it is not oppressive. The nights are nearly always cool and once one enters the hill districts one is struck by the remarkable difference in temperature; a difference of only a few hundred feet is sufficient to cause the thermometer to fall considerably. Although situated slightly off the main steamship routes, Java can easily be reached from Singapore by the fast luxurious steamers of the K.P.M. (Royal Packet Navigation Co.) and the magnificent European Steamers of the Netherland- and Rotterdam Lloyd-Royal Dutch Mail Lines in 36 hours and the trip itself is one of undying interest, passing as one does countless islands set in a tropical sea of varying hues.

Yet another Javanese idyll, seen through the lens of an unknown colonial photographer: fishing boats on a clear, still lake. Although in their haste to extract the maximum possible profit from their East Indian possessions, the Dutch colonial authorities frequently destroyed traditional livelihoods and cultures along with the environment, many of the colonists were simultaneously fascinated by the beauty of Indonesia.

Java's volcanoes brood over an impossibly crowded landscape. How so much humanity has managed to coexist alongside nature's most violent features is part of this island's magic. The photographer of this picture managed to capture that most awe-inspiring of all landscapes, majestic Mount Bromo in East Java, in the 1920s.

SUMATRA

The large, gourd-shaped island of Sumatra has acted for centuries as a conduit of culture and great wealth between the rest of the region and the world beyond. Yet from above its largely untamed and often forbidding landscape, few suggestions of the land's ancient significance are visible. Facing the western world at its northern end, and dipping towards the east at the other, Sumatra was well-placed to become an early centre of commerce in the region. To this favourable position were added the bountiful resources of the island's forests. It is hardly surprising that by the sixth century A.D., Sumatran products had begun to displace those of Persia as the main imports of the Chinese empire.

A noted authority on Southeast Asian history, D.G.E. Hall, has attributed the rise of the great empire of Srivijaya, on the southeastern coast of Sumatra, to the Malay seafarers who developed early trade links between peninsular Asia, the Indonesian archipelago and the Indian subcontinent. Contemporary inscriptions attest to Srivijaya's hegemony over at least a dozen ports and principalities in the region by the late seventh century. All ships passing through the Straits of Malacca were forced to call at the empire's ports, where a duty was levied upon their cargoes. The Sailendra dynasty that ruled Srivijaya also played a key role in the spread of Buddhism to Java.

Strangely, though, while much of their heritage was bequeathed to Java in the form of lasting and massive monuments to their religion, there is almost no trace of the great Sailendrians and their empire of Srivijaya on Sumatra. As Hall puts it, 'So far as history is concerned, unheralded they come and unheralded they go.' No-one even knows precisely where Srivijaya was located, though educated guesswork places its site somewhere close to the modern city of Palembang. Srivijaya's apparently total effacement is accounted for by the theory that the city was constructed mainly of wood—these energetic seafarers having, perhaps, little use for more enduring buildings of stone or brick, whose construction would have required large amounts of time and labour. Also, the marshy lowlands of Sumatra's eastern littoral may have been too soft to support the necessary foundations. If the theory is correct, the physical remains of the city would quickly have rotted to nothing following the collapse of the empire in the thirteenth century.

Perhaps the old capital of Srivijaya was a metropolis rather like nineteenth-century Palembang, which Alfred Wallace described as a city of archetypal Malays, 'never building a house on dry land if they can find water to set it in, and never going anywhere on foot if they can reach the place in a boat.'

Having paved the way for so much of Southeast Asia's

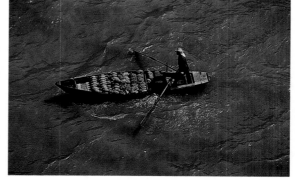

A fire opens a wound in the vast expanse of Sumatra's tropical forest, preceding pages. Fires can cause extensive damage to the primary forest and affect climatic conditions by sending up smoke particles which block out the sun for weeks. Left, a boatman rows his load of fruit through choppy waters on the way to market.

The Malay Muslim
Sultans of Siak may
have been descendants
of Hindu-Buddhist
kings, rulers of the
thirteenth-century
empire of Srivijaya.
Even if the two cultures
were not directly
linked, the semi-aquatic
nature of both hinted at
a certain continuity.
Throughout south
Sumatra, the
relationship between
man and the rivers he
lives by remains strong.
Substitute a temple for
the mosque, timber and
thatch for corrugated
tin, and the village of
Sri Indrapura probably
differs little from its
Srivijayan forbears.

Friday prayers at Medan's main mosque. The faithful overflow the building, their short prayer rugs spread before them, and all heads turn in prayer towards Mecca. The mosque is a survivor from the nineteenth-century Sultanate of Deli. Tombs of the faithful lie on the southward side of the mosque.

cultural and commercial development in the period before colonialism, Sumatra diminished in importance under Dutch rule, becoming scarcely more than a well-stocked larder of natural resources. At first spices were the chief export; in later years, rubber and oil headed the list of the island's natural bounties.

Customary chaos at the Pekenbaru minibus terminal. The buses are general-purpose transport in Java and Sumatra; they are often the only means by which rural villagers can bring their produce to market.

With the exploitation of resources having replaced trade as the major pursuit of man on Sumatra, efforts to tame the island's vast interior began in earnest. Planters and prospectors began making their way inland from the coast, following in the footsteps of explorers armed with machetes. By the nineteenth century, the word 'Sumatra' was synonymous with 'plantation'. For a while, the island became the world's largest producer of rubber. Rich inland oilfields were discovered along the east coast; in the years following independence, these were to provide an important source of prosperity for the fledgling Republic of Indonesia.

Trade and the later primacy of its exports helped turn Sumatra into a melting-pot of races, adding to its already diverse cultural composition. Today, Chinese, Indians, Arabs, and Javanese contribute to a very cosmopolitan society of some 35 million people. While most Javanese towns can boast some Chinese and a few families of Arab stock, the city of Medan in Northern Sumatra differentiates between Acehnese, Bataks, Malays, Javanese and Indians.

In the west of the island, the distinctive Minangkabau people live in coconut-tree-shrouded villages on the borders of their ricefields, preserving a unique, matrilineal culture in the face of a long history of outward migration. Their distinctive horn-roofed houses complement a landscape already blessed with abundant natural beauty.

North of Sumatra, the proud Acehnese add a distinctive touch of spice to the ethnic melting-pot. Haughty and fiercely defensive of their long tradition of cosmopolitan links with the outside world, Aceh is known as Serambi Islam, the 'veranda of Islam', because it was here that the predominant faith of modern Indonesia first took root. The Acehnese are proud of their resistance to Dutch rule, having fought a long and bloody war against the colonists.

Modern Sumatra, with its enormous natural resources, remains the cornucopia of the nation. Oil and rubber are still the two principal exports, though spices, hardwoods, tea, and a myriad other commodities contribute to the island's balance of trade. Northern and southern Sumatra are dotted with vast estates, neatly ordered expressions of man's conquest of the landscape. Yet much of Sumatra remains untamed, and the prospect of a sudden change in this state of affairs seems unlikely. For the time being at least, Sumatra's ancient cultural and economic might remains in abeyance. The focus of human activity in the archipelago has moved eastward, to the island next door.

Medan, the
capital of North
Sumatra, grew to
prominence in the
nineteenth century
as a centre serving
the Dutch plantation
economy, but it does
have a legacy of
independence under
the Sultanate of Deli.
Like the Grand Mosque
on page 30, the late
nineteenth century
sultan's palace, the
Istana Maimoon,
is a fine example of
the architectural style
popular in the old
Sultanate.

The last sultan of the South Sumatran principality of Siak was dethroned by a popular uprising in 1946—fittingly, perhaps, since a new Republic of Indonesia was born that year. His palace dates from the eighteenth century, a rare, well preserved example of the old Malay architecture, which mimicked Arabian styles while assuming European architectural conventions.

Clear, glassy smooth waters ringed with lush green hills make Lake Toba a favourite with visitors. But there is another side to Toba. The lake is also home to the region's Batak people. The simplicity of local life, as shown in this photograph, offers yet another example of how modern ways and the intrusions of outsiders appear to have had little impact on local ways of life in Indonesia.

The central focus of social life in most Sumatran villages, the mosque, is usually the biggest and most elaborate building as well. In rural areas, however, expensive materials are hard to come by or beyond the villagers' means. The rusted corrugated roofing of this tin mosque enhances rather than detracts from its charm.

The deep hues of Sumatra's rivers reflect not just their depth, but also the wealth of natural material they carry, swept off their banks from the forest that blankets much of this island. Settlements such as this one flourish on the riverbanks, reflecting the traditional importance of rivers in the Malay world as highways and sources of sustenance.

This typical riverside town reveals the consociation of religions in Indonesian society. Visible here: a mosque, a church and a Chinese temple. The Indonesian tradition of religious tolerance is actively fostered by a government which recognizes the devastating potential of religious and ethnic conflict in a society where so many different races and creeds live in close proximity with one another.

The vast storage tanks at the Caltex refinery testify to Sumatra's enormous mineral wealth. The petroleum industry has provided the capital for much of Indonesia's development since the end of the colonial era. Refineries like this one process Sumatran crude oil and gas into a variety of petroleum products, adding value to the raw resource before export.

The Dutch found oil in Sumatra in the nineteenth century, but it was only after independence that commercial exploitation began in earnest. By the 1970s, oil was Indonesia's primary export and the economy depended on it to an extent which was recognized as unhealthy; oil revenues were ploughed back into the domestic economy in order to develop other industries with export potential. The policy has been successful. Today, oil refineries are producing as much for Indonesia's rapidly growing domestic market as for export.

The dense and infinitely varied forest canopy and the valuable logs it yields make Sumatra one of the last great storehouses of natural wealth in Southeast Asia. With resources on more densely populated islands like Java approaching the point of diminishing returns, the importance of this wealth, on Sumatra, Kalimantan and other relatively uncrowded islands, increases daily.

From above, Sumatra's greenery plays tricks on the eye. An island of green set in a lake glows like an undersea coral, a belt of forest looks for all the world like so many heads of broccoli. The sheer extent of the forest cover causes the viewer to search for points of reference with which to establish a perspective; even minor features assume an exaggerated degree of importance.

Elephants still roam the forests of Sumatra in sizeable numbers, though they have disappeared from almost every other part of the archipelago. In fact, attacks on remote villages by bands of wild elephants are not uncommon, and a school to tame the beasts has been set up in south Sumatra to overcome the problem. However, the elephants do not constitute nearly as great a menace to people and the environment as do the fires which regularly afflict the Sumatran forest. When these spread out of control, as they did most spectacularly during the prolonged dry season of 1991, the skies from here to Singapore and even the neighbouring Malayan peninsular are affected by a severe smoke haze.

Little remains of the ancient, mercantile, maritime empire of Srivijaya, which flourished on the east coast of Sumatra during the thirteenth century. The trading state hugged the coast of Riau, living off the sea—and on top of it, in what are thought to have been wooden water-towns on stilts.

Relics of Sumatra's Hindu-Buddhist past do remain, however, testifying to the early contact between India and Sumatra. There is also considerable evidence of contact between the cultures of Sumatra and the great Hindu-Buddhist empires of Java during Indonesia's classic period.

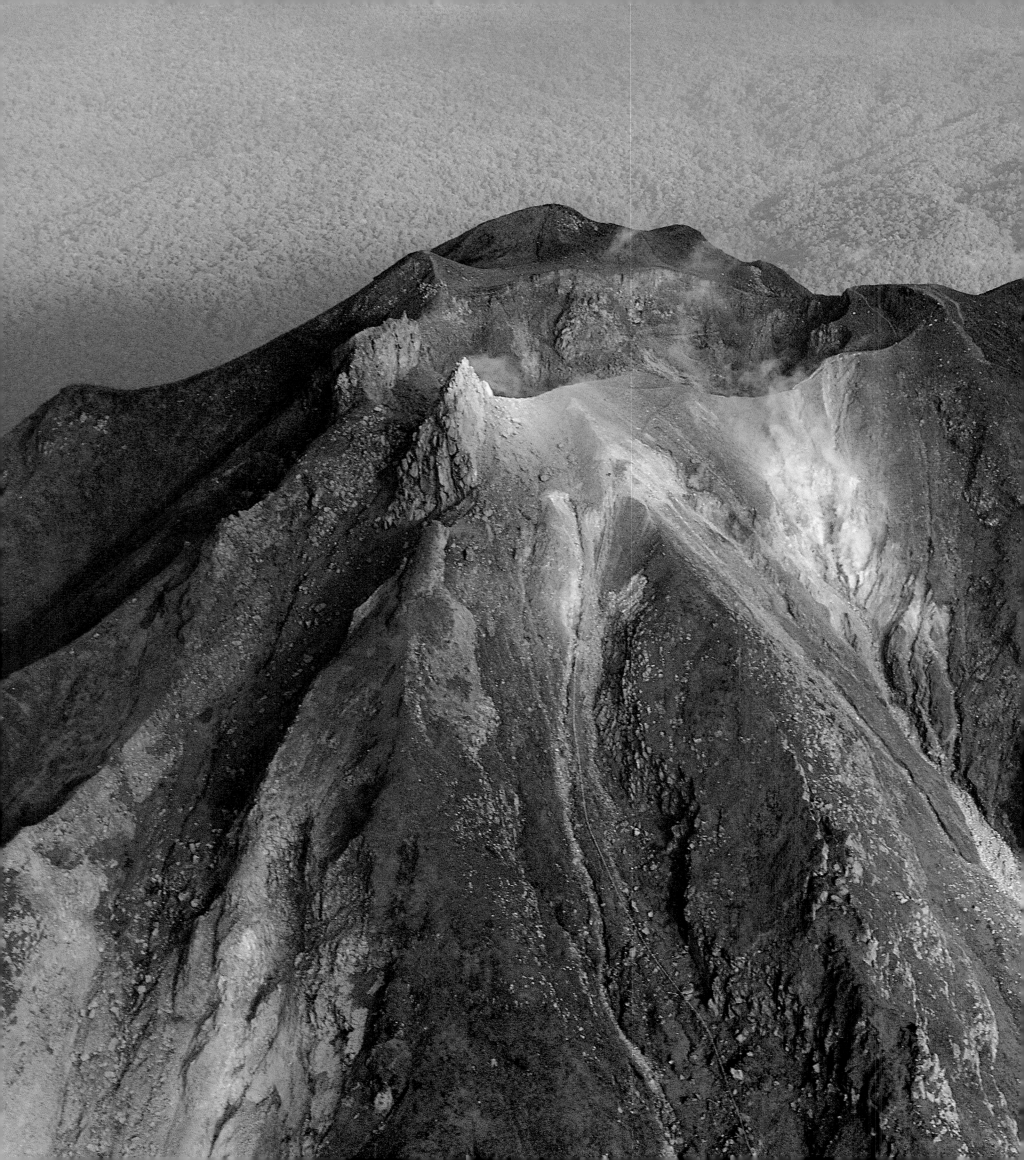

Dormant but menacing, a volcanic cone towers above the lush forest plain below. Most minor eruptions will threaten only the upper slopes, after which the carpet of green creeps once more up to the crater's edge. Life on a Sumatran plantation is tidy and ordered, following pages. These workers' houses offer only simple comforts, but Indonesia has come a long way from the harshness and exploitation of the colonial era. Lush green tea-bushes, some of them decades old, offer their tender leaves to this band of tea-pickers, pp. 50–51. The pickers cover themselves not to ward off the cooler breezes of these hill plantations, but to protect their skins from the sun.

JAVA

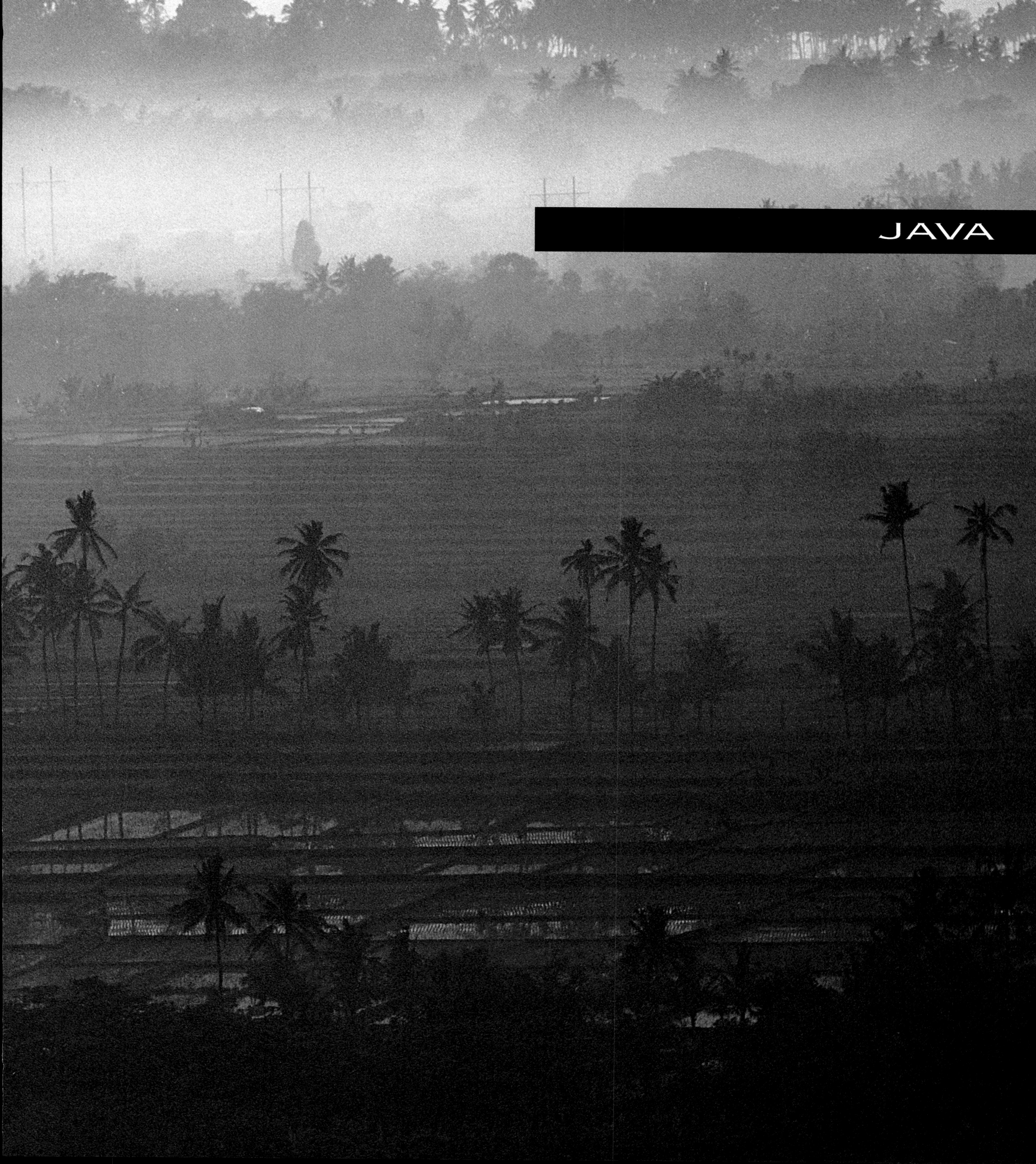

As if painted by a master artist, the morning mist defines the perspective on a typical Javanese scene, preceding pages. A volcano, left, one of thirty active cones on the island, is no less typical; there is hardly a spot anywhere in Java where at least one is not in view. The greatest of them all, Mount Bromo, broods over the peaceful fields and villages of East Java, its divinities placated by annual sacrifices to forestall the devastating eruption which would otherwise certainly take place.

Java, ethereal, wreathed in mystery, holds more than the traveller could discover in a lifetime. Yet at first sight, the prospect of dull, glassy marshland that defines its northern shores gives little indication of the enormous human and natural riches the island has to offer. This is the first of Java's many deceptions. Prone to ground-hugging mists and carpeted in seemingly endless greenery, the apparently spacious, rustic landscape looks nothing at all like what it is—the world's most densely inhabited island. Java is just 1200 kilometres long and five hundred wide, accounting for only seven percent of the total land area of Indonesia, but it is home to over sixty percent of Indonesia's population.

The island's demographic history is unique. Its population increased tenfold in the period between 1815 and 1930, from some 3.5 million to 36 million. Today the figure is more like a hundred million souls, a teeming, bustling mass of humanity. Flanking the arterial roads is an almost uninterrupted chain of settlement, and traffic along those roads is practically unceasing. Cities blend into towns, villages into one another. A beach deserted on weekdays will be brimming with locals at the weekend. Buses and minibuses easily outnumber private cars in rural areas.

Gazing over a land so marked by man yet still so graced by nature, one feels compelled to learn the secrets of its past. Fossils of primitive humans have been found in the region around the Solo River, suggesting that bands of the world's earliest hunter-gatherers once roamed the area. Artifacts found along with the remains suggest that, nearly a million years ago, these ancient hunters already possessed the beginnings of a culture. Local myths speak of migrations from mainland Asia, which brought with them first bronze-working techniques, then rice. The island, with its exceptional fertility, was perfect for rice cultivation. A dependable food supply fostered the development of the earliest Javanese kingdoms. Meanwhile trade developed along the coast, bringing these kingdoms into contact with those of the Indian subcontinent. Hinduism came to Java. Local rulers adopted the new religion, both to distinguish themselves from their people and to reinforce the rigid social hierarchy demanded by a rice-growing culture.

On Java, the Hindu model of the universe found an almost perfect reflection in nature. The chain of active volcanoes strung across the island presents a visible analogue of the mythical Mount Meru, the central point of Hindu cosmology. In the shadow of one of the biggest and most unpredictable of these volcanoes, Merapi, the kingdom of Mataram was established in the eighth century A.D., at a site close to the modern city of Yogyakarta. It was to be the first of several Hindu and Buddhist kingdoms of the

A hard day's work for these Javanese fishermen, who have to haul in their catch hand-over-hand from the tiny deck of their gaily-painted fishing boat.

From the hardwood timbers used in the building of these graceful ships to the planks used to unload their cargoes of sawn timber, it is very apparent that much of the inter-island trade in the archipelago continues to revolve around the natural bounty of its forests.

island. Among the titles assumed by later rulers of Mataram was one which described the king as 'the nail of the world' and 'the one who holds the world. It seems clear that the Javanese assimilated the Hindu view of the universe very completely.

All hands on deck to secure a load. Modern machinery and cranes are not available at all of Indonesia's ports, so much work still has to be done by hand.

Just to the east of Yogyakarta lies Prambanan, the largest surviving Hindu temple complex on Java, built some time between the eighth and tenth centuries A.D. and reconstructed from rubble during the present one. The detailed sculptures adorning the shrines to the Hindu trinity of Brahma, Vishnu and Siva are almost as vivid as those decorating the nearby Buddhist edifice of Borobudur, and in common with the latter, they reflect a society in which myth was as immediate as reality.

Central Javanese culture remains steeped in mysticism. The ancient sultanate survives, retaining the division into three royal houses imposed by the Dutch. The Sultans of Solo and Yogyakarta command cultural as well as spiritual authority. When Hamengkubuwono IX died in 1988, millions thronged the route to the royal burial grounds at Imogiri to pay their last respects. The old Sultan is also venerated as a hero of the revolution against the Dutch.

Decades of progress and modern development have left their mark, but much remains unchanged. The Javanese are still a deeply spiritual people, as close to their religion—whether they be Muslim or Christian—as they are to ancient spiritual beliefs. They combine religious tolerance with devotion to these beliefs, but underneath there is also, perhaps, an element of unpredictability. The writer and Catholic pastor Y.B. Mangunwijaya wrote of his people in a novel, The Weaverbirds, that 'the people of Java are little different from the mountainous island on which they reside, a chain of volcanoes which at any moment can awaken to cough up a phlegm of burning lava.'

Earlier this century, Augusta De Wit described Java as 'an enchanted garden', and spoke of the 'constant intrusion of the poetic, the legendary, the fanciful into the midst of reality'. The interplay of myth and reality finds expression in the well-known but not easily understood wayang shadow play. Perhaps too easily, the wayang has become a commonplace metaphor for contemporary Indonesian culture and politics.But while many Javanese may consciously emulate the heroes of the legend, their island is today the heart of a modern, urbanizing nation. Expressways snake across the padi fields, housing estates reach out from the cities to the rural fringe. Strategically placed industrial complexes, petrochemical plants and oil refineries provide employment and a new way of life for increasing numbers of rural Javanese, who flock to the cities and towns in search of jobs. Tradition blends easily with modernity, however. For the Javanese, their culture and the land it inhabits are a timeless source of strength.

At the centre of the traditional Javanese community stands the mosque. Here the twin minarets are fashioned very much like lighthouses, veritable beacons of faith. Every day at dawn and dusk, the soothing sound of chanted verses from the Koran may be heard over the sounds of daily life, reasserting the preeminence of Islam in the minds of the faithful.

Although Indonesia as a whole is self-sufficient in rice, the island of Java, with its hundred million mouths, must import food to keep them from hunger. Java is so heavily populated that it simply cannot feed itself. Ricefields, like the recently harvested ones above, are among the most recurrent features of the landscape; in fact, at least half of Java's land area is under cultivation. Yet the annual deficit remains, and will probably do so for the forseeable future.

By no means all
of Java is under rice.
The crops for which the
island used to be best
known were those
grown on a commercial
basis on the large
Dutch plantations:
coffee, cocoa and
spices of different sorts.
Among the latter were
cloves, which continue
to be produced in vast
quantities to feed the
demand for kretek,
the clove-flavoured
cigarettes so popular
in Indonesia.

Flat plains strewn with every conceivable form of cultivation reflect the richness of Java's volcanic soils. Not one square metre is neglected. Even the boundaries of fields yield a rich crop of bananas; the river banks are covered by vegetable plots. Verdant and always well-tended, Java's agricultural patchwork belies the farmers' hard efforts to keep the land tame and productive.

A portrait of how life is sustained on the world's most densely populated island: earth and man in perfect harmony, ricefields fitting snugly against compact villages like a well-designed jigsaw. The suggestion of timelessness in these pictures is supported by the facts of life among the Javanese, for whom the pace of events is very much dictated by 'natural time': the diurnal cycle, the precession of tides and equinoxes, the turning seasons—rather than by inflexible schedules based on clocks and calendars.

Nothing seems as serene as a Javanese village. As orderly, when seen from the air, as are the patterns that govern daily life under its roofs and out in its fields, the Javanese desa is looked upon as the model of village life in Indonesia. The neatness of the whitewashed wattle-and-brick dwellings matches the scrupulously maintained ricefields, whose luxuriant fertility in the days before chemical fertilizers ensured some of the highest yields anywhere in the world.

For this Javanese fishing community, the natural way to preserve food for storage is to harness the sun's energy. Traditional staple fare consists of rice, chili and a little dried fish. While there is nothing insanitary about the arrangement, the aroma around these villages must be inhaled to be believed.

Java's low-lying, muddy northern coastline looks grim and desolate, yet it offers a bountiful harvest of fish and shrimp. Fishing boats, pages 70-71, will trawl the coastal waters by night, using lamps to attract the fish, while during the day, the fishermen cast their nets by hand for fingerlings. The island of Madura, with its long south coast facing Java, is famous for its hardy fishermen. At low tide, their proud little boats rest close to the village, above; children potter for crabs in the tidal sands.

The scene is ageless, a definitive perspective on the intimate Javanese bond between land and water. A coastal creek near the North Javanese town of Cirebon shelters the graceful fishing boats which haul in protein from the sea to balance the stodgy rice diet. Nearby, bunded mud-flats hold fish ponds, which when drained turn into handy salt pans.

Much of
Indonesian life
revolves around
collective activity.
On Java, this means
providing the space
for enormous numbers
of people to gather;
stadia, fields, even
car parks are pressed
into service for
parades and pageants.
Here in the Central
Javanese court city
of Solo, better known
as Surakarta, bright
trappings laid out
in an open compound
tell of a festival
about to begin.

A sports field near Bandung prepares for a parade. Like so many toy soldiers on a board, the serried ranks form up with disciplined precision. The Indonesian armed forces have no easy task, for the land they protect is sprawling, patchily inhabited and features some of the world's most varied environments. Indonesian soldiers must expect to be called upon to fight in teeming jungles, sheer mountainous terrain, marshland, mangrove swamp, semi-desert and, of course, on water.

On top of Borobudur. The monument echoes the classic Hindu-Buddhist concept of the universe: a mandala of concentric topographies focused on a lofty central mountain or summit, the pinnacle of creation. Its proportions are ideal; all elements of the cosmos are in harmony with one another. With its basalt blocks amazingly unweathered by time, the permanence of Borobodur stands as testimony to the strength of an earlier civilization.

Appearing almost toylike from this perspective, the greatest monument of Java's classic period rises above the Central Javanese plain. Borobudur is perhaps best known for the reliefs which decorate its walls and galleries from its upper 'plateau' all the way down to the 'hidden foot', which consists of a band of carving running around the uppermost layer of the foundations of the building, buried and invisible. The carvings illustrate Jataka, tales of the Buddha in previous incarnations, the Lalitavistara, the story of his birth, and the Gandavyuha, a Buddhist parable of the quest for enlightenment.

JAKARTA

Tracing a crazy-quilt pattern on the urban landscape, Jakarta's red-tiled urban kampong still hold out despite the onslaught of modernity, preceding pages. Even among the narrow streets and closely-packed houses, a web of communities remains bound tightly to a formal village system, left: the mosque surrounded by houses, the classic pattern of the Javanese rural community, is repeated here.

apital cities generally reflect the soul of the nation they govern, and Jakarta is no exception. The sprawling urban expanse perched on Java's northwest coast is known to Indonesians as Ibu Kota, or Mother City. While most of its 7.5 million inhabitants are relatively recent city-dwellers and the majority are immigrants from neighbouring Javanese provinces, most of Indonesia's ethnic groups are nonetheless represented by sizeable communities within the city.

Ibu Kota is very much the nation's focus. From six o'clock in the morning onwards, a passenger can fly from Jakarta airport to almost every one of Indonesia's twenty-seven provincial capitals. Buses connect the city to far-flung destinations in Java and Sumatra. Indonesia's regional shipping lanes are among the most densely travelled in the world; the main port of arrival and departure is Jakarta. Most administrative, financial and political functions fan out from the city, and few decisions are made anywhere in the country without the matter first being referred there.

The Dutch built Jakarta—known during the colonial period as Batavia—in the image of their own canal-cleft cities. They were able to do so by chancing upon a site as flat and marshy as any in the Low Countries. Healthy it was not. The early seventeenth-century Dutch Governor, General Jan Pieterzoon Coen, sacrificed thousands of native lives to drain the malarial marshes at the mouth of the Ciliwung River, around which the city of Batavia was built.

Here, in 1618, the Dutch established their first permanent settlement, in the form of a fortified stone building. Sultan Agung, paramount ruler of Java, described it as 'a thorne in the foot, which I must take pains to pluck out, for fear the whole body should be endangered.' As good as his word, the Sultan laid siege to the fort in 1629 with an army of some two hundred thousand men. The Dutch defences amounted to a few hundred soldiers and some cannon; malaria and a shortage of food almost certainly accounted for the Sultan's failure to dislodge them. The 'thorne' remained firmly in place, and the whole body eventually succumbed to the colonial infection it spread.

By the late nineteenth century, Batavia was the archetypal Southeast Asian colonial metropolis: a modern city by Asian standards, the administrative centre of Dutch rule over the huge archipelago. Horse-drawn trams provided transport, gaslights illuminated its spacious tree-lined streets. Covering most of the area known today as Merdeka Square was an expanse of wooded parkland, the 'Koningsplein.' 'It is best described as a system of parks and avenues,' wrote Augusta De Wit of the city in the early 1900s, 'linked by many a pleasant byway and shadowy path, with here and there a glimpse of the Betawai

Timeless masters of the inter-island seas, Bugis prahus line up at the quayside to unload their cargoes.

Like a massive flywheel, Jakarta's Jalan Thamrin roundabout sends the rush-hour traffic speeding along the main north-south axis of the city. In the lower left foreground the city's first multi-story hotel, the Hotel Indonesia, which dates from the 1960s, is now dwarfed by the newer and much larger Hyatt.

Canal gliding along between the bamboo groves on its banks, and everywhere the whiteness of low, pillared houses, standing well back from the road, each in its own leafy garden.'

Many of these low, pillared houses with their thick stuccoed walls and graceful red-tiled roofs have survived to grace today's Jakarta. Further north, a long row of dilapidated buildings with characteristic Dutch profiles suggests scenes from Amsterdam. However, much of colonial Batavia has been erased; the Hotel Des Indes, for example, a landmark of the Dutch period, fell victim to the planning zeal of the sixties and seventies.

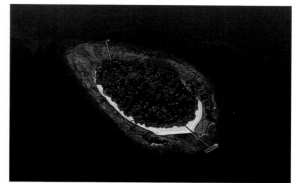

Echoing the shape of the roundabout opposite, an islet in the Pulau Seribu group provides a vibrant contrast in almost every other sense. The group lies not far off the coast of Jakarta, and many of the islands have been developed as resorts.

From above, the city's elegant new steel and glass towers suggest an archipelago of modernity in a sea of the past. The aerial prospect is still dominated by the red roofs of densely-packed urban villages, whose narrow lanes trace a disorderly but nevertheless organized pattern. Under these roofs lives the vast majority of Jakarta's people.

On the ground each such village has distinct administrative and social boundaries, fostering security and a sense of mutual support, a rural tradition which thrives in the urban setting. Dusk in these urban kampong brings out a host of hawkers and food-sellers, pushing their carts and announcing their wares with a distinctive cry or the beat of a gong. Sweeping over and across the kampong are multi-lane expressways and toll roads, which allow some respite from the choking traffic of older city routes. Along with the expressways, a host of offices, apartments, secondary roads and even golf courses are slowly paring Jakarta's urban villages back to the fringes of the city.

The central business district has grown rapidly and spectacularly in the past five years. Large vacant lots, previously abandoned to squatters and their small market-gardens, have been replaced by the thrusting symbols of Indonesia's new corporate giants. This prosperity has inevitably brought changes to the rhythm of the city.

Fleets of limousines compete with an armada of buses in the daily crush on the highway; pedicabs which once roamed the main streets have been restricted to the outer suburbs. Wet markets are being replaced by air-conditioned supermarkets, and traditional stall food is facing competition from western fast-food outlets. For the time being these contrasting lifestyles coexist, offering a unique contradiction and a metaphor for Indonesia's present stage of growth: one foot in the future, the other planted firmly in the past. Just as the juxtaposition of Jakarta's main mosque and cathedral symbolizes the country's religious syncretism, so the few steps from the poor neighbourhood of Tanah Abang to the foot of the glass and steel wall lining Jalan Thamrin, the city's principal thoroughfare, suggests that the gulf between past and future, like other divisions, is bridged by Indonesia's enduring passion for unity.

The old mirrored in the new. One side of this new multi-story bank building reflects the urban village of Pejampongan. Another side of the building looks down on Jakarta's central landmark; the Semanggi clover-leaf interchange. Formerly, two major routes met at a level intersection here, causing legendary traffic-jams. Now, for most of the day at least, traffic flows smoothly.

Jakarta's main Istiqlal mosque and Santa Ursula cathedral share a central location, side by side as a testament to Indonesia's tradition of religious tolerance. Just beyond the mosque is the Monas monument that occupies Merdeka Square. Together they symbolize the essential aspirations of this city of twelve million people, but are fast being dwarfed by the phalanx of modern office buildings which define the rapid growth of the city's central business district over the past five years.

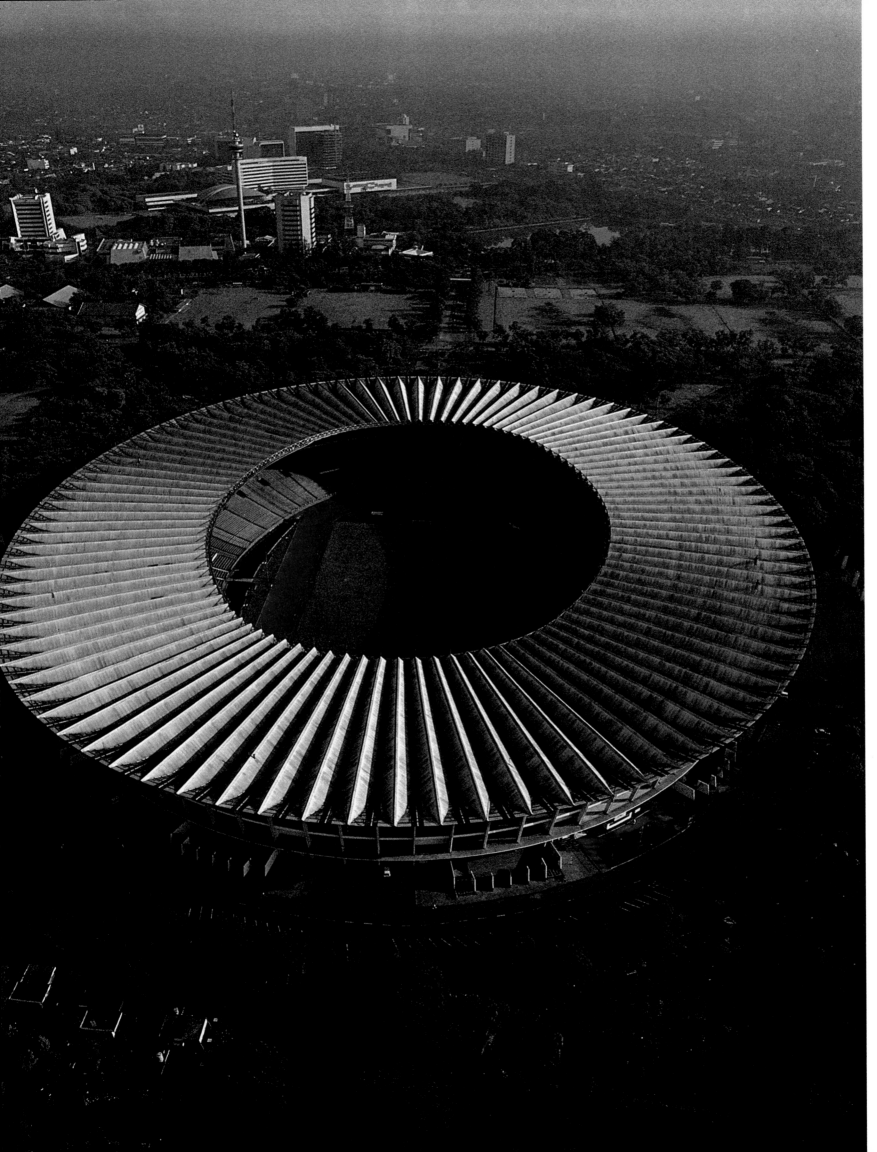

Built by Sukarno on a characteristically grand scale, Jakarta's main stadium at Senayan was a considerable architectural challenge. In the background, just behind the TV transmission tower, sit the national assembly buildings, another legacy of the Sukarno period, and the focus of Indonesia's formal political process.

Jakarta is full of architectural oddities. Here the science and technology museum assumes the look of a modern airport terminal, with a retired stalwart of the national airline parked nearby. Jakarta is full of museums. The National Museum, originally the Museum of the Batavian Society for the Arts and Sciences, contains superb examples of Hindu-Buddhist art and a trove of ethnographic objects, housed in premises as distinctive (if less eyecatching) than those pictured above.

Progress and modernity have yet to drown out the neighbourhood call to prayer in Jakarta. Nonetheless, should competition for urban space infringe on the city's spiritual needs, there is always the option to build upward, as the designers of this downtown mosque clearly discovered.

Five times a day, loudspeakers atop this minaret will broadcast the call to prayer, a call to the faithful that is one of the most distinctive sounds of Jakarta, heard even above the modern din of traffic and blaring horns. Along the narrow streets of the neighbourhood, those answering the call will stroll, their prayer rugs slung over their shoulders, in sandal-shod feet; it is a time to wash off the grime of the city and kneel in contemplation within the cool interior of the mosque.

Incongruously symmetrical, almost like an eighteenth-century English landscaped garden, Jakarta's Taman Mini offers the visitor a sampling of the wide variety of sights found in the archipelago. It is a kind of museum, an attempt to present in miniature, in an ordered, edited form, a diversity almost too large to be comprehended.

A tale of two cities. On one side of Jakarta's orbital toll road lies a densely packed urban village. The golf course on the other is a sign of the times, catering to the increasing numbers of those upwardly mobile members of Jakarta's mercantile classes who like to play a round of golf before heading for the office early in the morning.

Jakarta's port area, left, betrays little sense of the present, with traditional sailing ships nestled in one of the city's older areas. The name of the harbour, Sunda Kelapa, harks back to the original spice-trading port that existed here before the coming of the Dutch— indeed, before the arrival of Islam in Java. An old Dutch godown, or warehouse, nearby has been converted into a museum preserving relics and models of the maritime activity that has taken place here for centuries. Loaded to the gunwales, these inter-island wooden freighters, above, disgorge their loads to nearby godowns buried in the maze of streets beyond the docks, where the pungent odours of spices and freshly-cut timber pervades the narrow alleyways.

A profusion of boats berthed at Sunda Kelapa, Jakarta's ancient harbour. A world apart from the city's modern skyline, the unchanging rhythm of inter-island trade and contact remains a vital, though often overlooked, component of the nation's economy. The unceasing activity of these waters carries an unmistakable stamp of the old world, but it is of urgent relevance to the daily life of modern Indonesia.

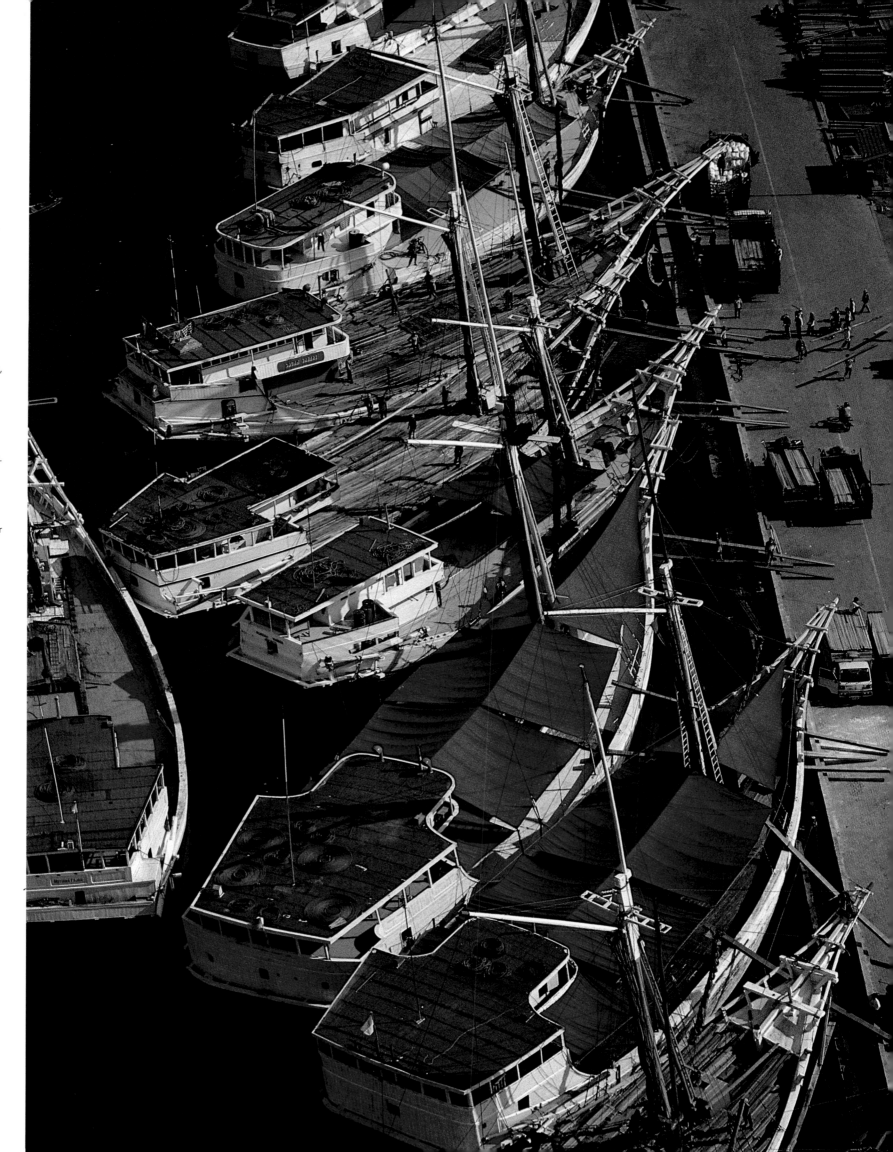

Perhaps nowhere in the world are there trading vessels more graceful and stately than these Buginese prahus moored at Sunda Kelapa. The ships have changed little over the centuries, their economical but sleek lines making the best possible compromise between fleetness and capacity. Prahus are still made of hardwood with traditional caulking. Sails are used together with modern diesel engines—and the cargo is still loaded and unloaded on the backs of sturdy longshoremen.

Skein-like flecks
of coral, some barely
breaking the surface
of the Java Sea,
the Pulau Seribu
or Thousand Islands
lie just 75km due north
from the effluent-stained
waters of Jakarta bay.
Many are uninhabited.
The larger islands
are home to fishing
communities, exploiting
the coral shoals
to supply fresh fish
to the capital.

While many of the Thousand Islands have been developed as hotels, others continue to support their traditional communities. The development of the islands has proceeded with some care; for example, none holds more than one hotel, though often the accommodation takes the form of chalets or cabanas. Visitors to the islands often find it hard to imagine that Jakarta is only a couple of hours away by boat.

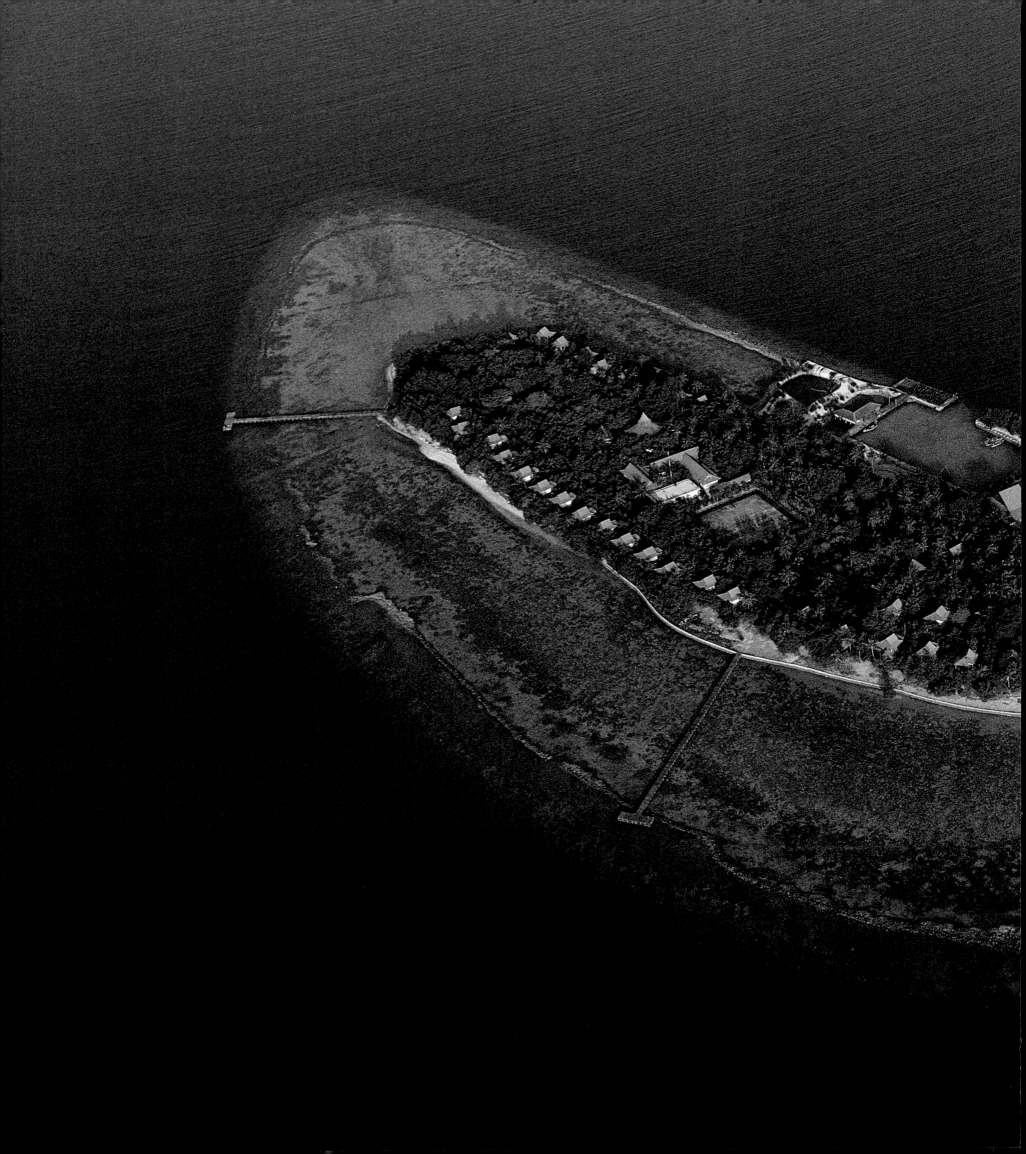

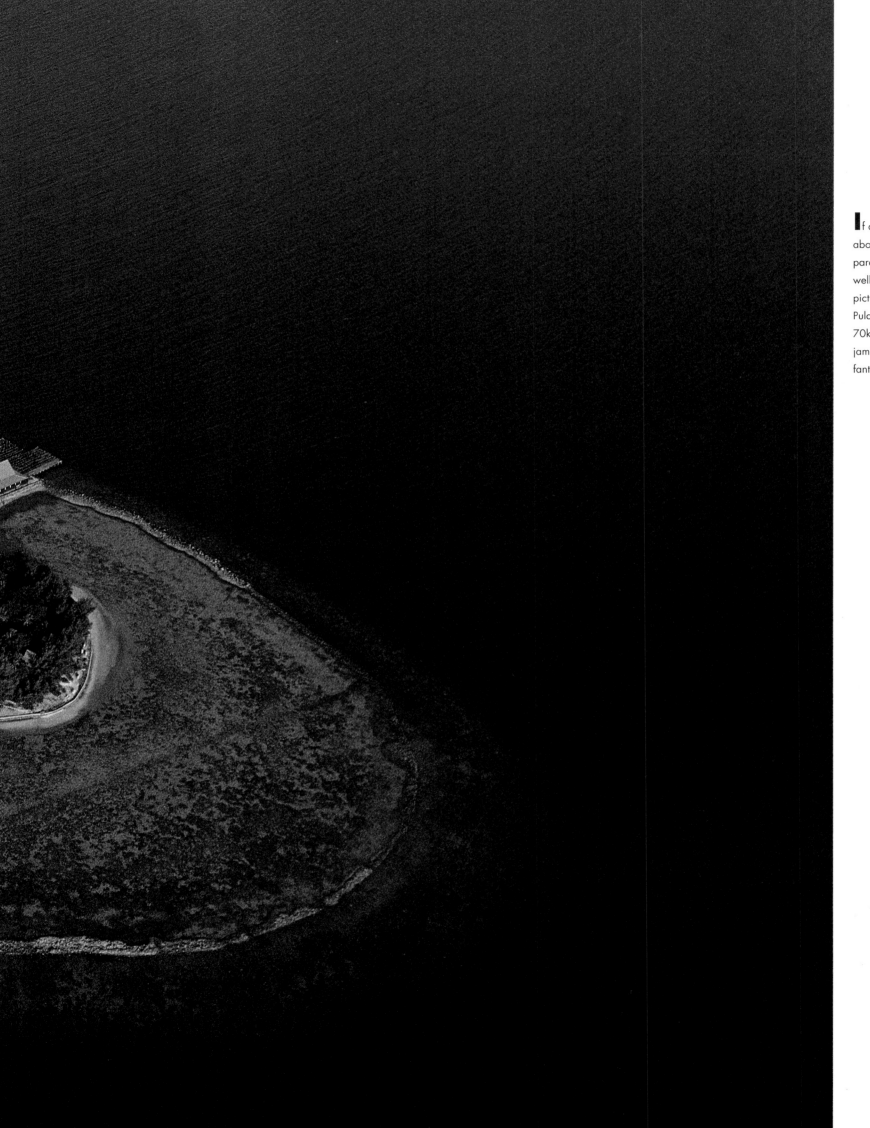

If asked to fantasise about a tropical island paradise, one might well describe such a picture as this—but in Pulau Seribu, only 70km from the traffic jams of Jakarta city, the fantasy comes true.

The territory of Indonesia is popularly known as Tanah Air, literally 'land and water'. On Java's intensely cultivated landscape, both elements are equally vital. In this flooded field not far from the capital, they blend to create an image of rich fertility.

BALI

Bali is many things to its many visitors, and most of these things are beautiful. Matchless Asian grace and artistic talent are here commingled with an easy charm: the result, like the setting, is a riot of tropical colour. But above all, Bali is a paradox. How such natural beauty in close partnership with an unfading culture has survived the concentrated onslaught of tourism is nothing short of a modern wonder. Most traditional cultures and environments require preservation; Bali's unique landscape and society seem almost to feed off their exposure to the contemporary world.

Adaptation comes naturally to the Balinese. Their pear-shaped volcanic home, often called the Island of the Gods, has been densely populated since ancient times. Over the centuries, the Balinese have grown so adept at altering their natural surroundings to their taste and livelihood that the results have themselves the aspect of nature. What from above seems an idyllic, almost virgin landscape is more often a complex artifact, fashioned for ritual use or reshaped to provide its inhabitants with the necessities of life. The only telltale signs of this transformation will be a Hindu temple on a rocky outcrop by the sea, or a series of rice terraces hugging the contours of the land. From the malleable chalks of Ulu Watu, used to fashion temple fixtures, to the myriad ceremonial uses of the palm frond, the Balinese have learned to rely on what nature has to offer, and remain reluctant to take up modern substitutes.

Historical continuity also helps to explain Bali's resilience in the face of change. Hindu influences and traditions of kingship probably spread from neighbouring Java to Bali in the eighth century A.D. The Javanese influence made itself felt more strongly after a succession of conquests by the expansionist rulers of East Java in the thirteenth and fourteenth centuries. Not long afterwards, Bali settled into a pattern distinguished by the rise and fall of competing regional rulers and princedoms, and thus immersed in its own affairs, was largely ignored by the outside world until the middle of the nineteenth century. The impact of Islam on the cultures of the rest of Indonesia was gentle and assimilative, but lasting and firmly decisive for all that; in Bali, by comparison, it has hardly been felt at all.

The Dutch began their conquest of Bali in the 1880s, a process which culminated in 1906 in a bloody war which destroyed the Balinese aristocracy and left the island bereft of its traditional rulers. The culture survived nevertheless, partly because the loss of Bali's independence coincided with the arrival of the Dutch liberals who were beginning to supplant hard-nosed merchants in the administration of the colonies. They were captivated by the elaborate Hindu religious ceremonies and their

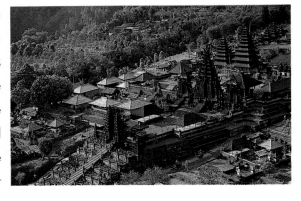

Sculpted over centuries, the Balinese terraced ricefield, preceding pages, appears as graceful as the delicate wooden carvings for which the island is famous. In a pattern so well conceived, every square inch of arable land can be planted. Left, Besakih temple at the foot of Gunung Agung, Bali's highest mountain.

Perfectly formed and locked together with almost inconceivable precision, these Balinese terraced ricefields are best viewed from above. Their beauty belies the vital role they play in supporting dense numbers of people in small areas. Yet the contours of these fields, their carefully maintained bunds, and the gravity-fed flow of water which irrigates them represent an enduring form of cultivation without which the population would suffer.

Like multicoloured water-bugs darting across the surface of a pond, these Balinese jukung boats hug the shoreline. Their long bamboo outriggers and highly-manoeuverable triangular sails evolved so that they could safely surmount the surf that pounds the island.

associated artistic expressions. By the 1930s, several European artists had made Bali their home. It was this artistic migration that paved the way for the island's exposure to the outside world.

The migrants were enchanted by Bali's tropical charm. Here, says the contemporary Dutch painter Arie Smit, 'Nothing is just ordinary. The soil is of excessive fertility. Plant growth is luxurious. The sky is peopled by refined creatures. The Sea is a menace. Peasants are graceful. Life is tranquil.' Just as the South Pacific islands exerted a strong fascination on French Impressionist painters, other European artists were drawn to the light and colour they found on Bali. 'Light in Bali is riotous,' says Arie Smit. 'Before it reaches the ground it is broken at all angles by tropical vegetation and bounced back in all directions by walls, roofs, water-pools, or the shiny skin of people and animals.' Even those who made only a brief visit were often greatly influenced by what they saw.

Encouraged to maintain their customs and forms of expression, and having little else to offer, the Balinese soon found their culture becoming a marketable resource. Crowds of holidaymakers followed on the heels of the artists, and as tourism developed after independence, the painters and sculptors of Bali gained fame and wealth. Latterly they have turned their skills to designing and moulding the features of new hotels and convention centres.

A model of the process is found not far from the capital city of Denpasar. The village of Ubud, set in a gently undulating landscape of rice fields, is populated by artists and artisans encouraged to settle there by European artists like Walter Spies. Finding a ready market for their productions among visitors and wealthy expatriate residents, they no longer needed to work the land. Today nearly all labour in Ubud is imported from Java, and the indigenous people are prosperous entrepreneurs. Outwardly, this charming town is a haven for the arts—painters and sculptors may be seen at work everywhere one turns. In reality, the existence of Ubud is compelling proof that tourism pays.

The other side of Bali—the tourism industry which sustains the island's economy—is not as ugly as some visitors like to make out. The hotels are for the most part elegantly designed and discreetly blended with the local landscape; there are few eyesores. Even the hotel bathrooms make full use of Balinese decor. The Balinese themselves have acquired a flair for the hotel and catering business, so much so that on neighbouring Lombok, where tourism is a more recent development, most of the hotels are staffed and run by Balinese. As they have done with the other natural resources of island, Bali's inhabitants have harmoniously adapted the beauty of their homeland to the service of their livelihood, without doing violence to that beauty, to themselves or to their culture.

This double bay is a famous landmark on the coast of Lombok, Bali's immediate eastern neighbour. Although the two islands are physically close to one another, they are scenically very different; Lombok's drier climate will not support as great a profusion of greenery as on Bali. However, Lombok's rugged countryside has its own attractions, not least of them Indonesia's second highest mountain, Mount Rinjani.

Tirtagangga water gardens. Living between the sea and the mountains, the Balinese regard water as an element of spiritual as well as material sustenance. Locals believe that spirits, benevolent or malefic, inhabit every nook and cranny of the island—which could explain why almost no part remains uncared for or untended.

The antique landscape of Central Bali seems a world away from the surf-and-sun image of the beach resorts to the south. In spite of the volume of tourist traffic that passes through the island every year, most such activity is confined to a relatively small area. For the majority of the people, tourism has brought prosperity without disrupting their traditional ways of life, or devaluing the rituals and customs which bind their society together so closely.

In spite of their idyllic appearance, the ricefields of Bali are the result of back-breaking labour. Mechanical contrivances are kept to a minimum; the farmers are conservative, and some of them fear that modern equipment, with its rumbling engines, puffing exhausts and glittering blades of steel, may offend or frighten away the goddess of fertility, Dewi Sri. Come harvest time, the rice must be gathered and threshed by hand on the spot. But like most activities on this island of almost three million people, the toil of the harvest is eased by the application of collective effort.

The rotational nature
of rice-farming offers
a kaleidoscope of
colour, varying from
area to area as well
as throughout the year.
In one field, the rice
is ready to harvest.
In the field adjoining,
the burnt stubble lies
on ground already
harvested. Elsewhere,
a lighter, almost
fluorescent shade of
green tells of young
rice shoots in their first
stage of growth.

A fertile tapestry of rice carpets Bali's gently undulating valleys. The shade of green is vivid, almost preternatural, yet few other landscapes are as soothing to the eye.

Ghostly volcanic cones offer a mountainous backdrop to villages inhabited by the ancient Aga people, remnants of the original non-Hindu inhabitants of Bali, whose arrival on the island predated that of the Javanese. The Aga were probably of Mongolian origin, similar (but not necessarily related) to the Toraja people of Sulawesi, further east. Preceding pages, the forbidding crater of Bali's highest and most sacred volcano, Mount Agung. Over 3,000 metres high, it last erupted in 1963. The volcano is also the spiritual focus of Balinese culture, and the traditional locus of the old kings' power. Near the foot of the volcano lies the island's most important temple, the Pura Besakih. Here Balinese come to draw strength from the powerful spirit that inhabits the mountain.

Mount Batur in northeast Bali shares its setting within the ancient remains of a much larger crater with a large freshwater lake which claims almost a third of the total area. In this region live the Aga, whose customs and rituals differ from those of the Hindu Balinese. The villagers of Trunyan, for example, have a custom of exposing their dead to the elements, and a graveyard near lake Batur is full of their skeletons.

The Balinese who follow the Hindu religion do so in a form very different from that of India. They have a creation myth which accounts for their own unique appearance, and their pantheon includes gods and goddesses with attributes unknown on the subcontinent; these are probably local folk deities who have assumed more majestic forms over time. The temples which dot the islands every few hundred metres are masterpieces in brick, stone and palm thatch: oases of spiritual calm.

Typically Balinese to turn something practical into a work of art. Here the undulating rice terraces of Ubud offer an idyllic setting for a hotel. One has to look twice before one realizes exactly what the complex of buildings is—at first glance it could be mistaken for a slightly-more-prosperous-than-usual village. The result of such tasteful handling is that Bali has been spared the despoliation large-scale tourism has inflicted in other places.

A Balinese farmer tending his field before sowing. The cool mud on which he treads will bear his weight, and that of a buffalo, but no more—otherwise, the hard pan holding the water will be ruptured. Practical considerations like these, along with the farmers' sense of their work as a form of spiritual activity, explains the lack of mechanization, and the need to do most of the work in the ricefields by hand. Nevertheless, harvests are bountiful; Dewi Sri rewards her people's devotion.

Reaping an ocean
harvest in the shallows
off the south coast of
Bali. These marine
farmers will eventually
send their nutritious
harvest of seaweed to
the Japanese market.

The southern tip of Bali elongates into a narrow isthmus which connects the chalk cliffs of the Bukit peninsula to the mainland. The peninsula, shaped like an upside-down miniature version of Bali itself, was once wilderness, the hunting grounds of the Rajas of Bali in the days before the mass suicide of the island's ruling dynasty in 1906. Ulu Watu, at the easternmost extremity of the peninsula, offers some of the most compelling views to be had on the island.

Guarded by snakes which inhabit the nearby caves and are thought by the Balinese to be the manifestation of semi-divine beings called nagas, Tanah Lot temple was founded by a wandering Hindu saint. The temple is isolated at high tide, and the erosion of the rock on which it stands bears witness to the ferocity of the surf which pounds at its base. At low tide, however, the waters recede, and the faithful pass to and fro with offerings to the gods.

The market opens as these Madurese fishing boats, heavily laden, reach Bali's shore. Not all areas are lucky enough to possess a cold storage facility, so the catch must be hauled quickly up the sands, divided up and sold as fast as possible. Like most productive activities in Bali, landing the catch is a great social occasion.

Mount Rinjani on Lombok, Bali's island neighbour, is the second highest peak in Indonesia. Every full moon night between April and October, the local people flock to what is actually an active volcano, believing that the steaming waters of its crater lake have tremendous healing power. At 3,800 metres, the summit of Rinjani is not easily attained. Visitors require police permits, guides, porters, sturdy shoes and plenty of warm clothing.

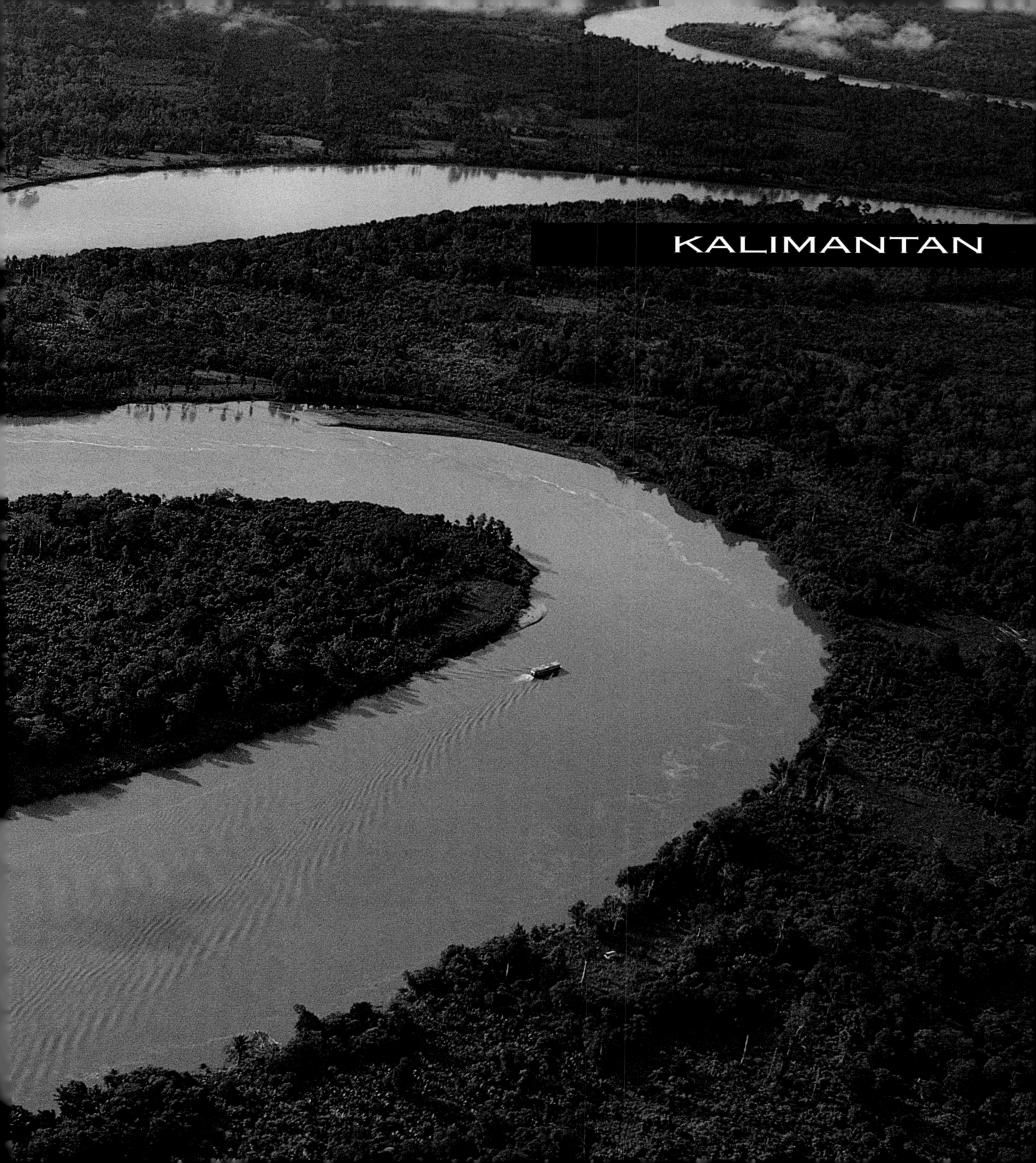

KALIMANTAN

**A**ccording to the folklore prevailing in the forested riverine lowlands of East Kalimantan, when a stranger comes upriver with good intentions, rain will fall even in the dry season. If the intentions are bad, no rain will fall at all. This belief says much about a part of Indonesia which has remained remote and inaccessible for much of its history. Two-thirds of Borneo, the third largest island in the world, is Indonesian territory. The Indonesian portion is divided into three provinces: East, Central and South Kalimantan. Together they are home to a population of some six million people, thinly scattered over a densely forested landscape penetrated only by a number of wide, muddy brown rivers.

From the air, the sense of almost limitless space is striking. Straddling the equator, the squat mass of Borneo is one of the world's largest expanses of tropical rainforest. The majestic dipterocarp trees rise a hundred metres from the jungle floor, presenting a dense green canopy to the sky. From a great height the canopy looks like a velvet carpet; it gives a misleading sense of hugging the ground, even along the mountainous ridges of the interior; the illusion persists until a lower view or a break in the canopy reveals the immense girth and height of some of the trees. Ochre yellow streaks in this otherwise unbroken green landscape are the only signs that man passes here. The streaks are access roads, obviously cut with a great deal of difficulty, to open up this rich source of hardwood timber.

In areas close to the coast, where tree-felling and cultivation have challenged the forest's sovereignty over the land, it is evident that nature is quickly regaining supremacy, recovering whatever ground it may have temporarily lost. The dense vines and shrubbery proliferate, taking advantage of the light before the canopy closes over them again. Although much forest has already been logged over in Kalimantan, it is somehow hard to imagine that nature will ever succumb to the onslaught of humanity—although this feeling can be a dangerous illusion, as the widespread destruction of environments across the globe has shown. Nonetheless, viewing Kalimantan from the air, one receives the distinct impression that the works of man will always remain a secondary feature in this landscape.

The indigenous people of this part of Borneo—Dayaks, Barito and Punan—mostly originate from nomadic forest gatherers of Austronesian stock, though Chinese, Malay and Filipino migrations over the centuries have made significant contributions to the genetic mix. The cultures of these indigenous peoples vary from one group to another, but common to them all was a belief that the spirit of a man continues to reside in his skull after death; this is the explanation behind the widespread practice of head-

Tracing a majestic, meandering furrow through the dense forests of East Kalimantan, the Mahakam River's brown waters, preceding pages, are the only route to the island's forbidding interior. The boatmen know every bend and shoal. Freshwater dolphins swim far inland up the Mahakam's deep waters. Left, a Bugis prahu moored at Samarinda waits to take on a cargo of timber.

Like crude brushstrokes on a plain canvas, these hardwood logs, already stripped of their bark, trace an orderly outline on their way to the sawmill. They have made their way down from the forest on trucks, but will make the last leg of their journey more gracefully, on the breast of the great Mahakam River.

In the novels and stories of Joseph Conrad the rivers of old Borneo were sources of darkness and mystery. On this minor tributary, no more menacing than any other village high street basking in the afternoon sunshine, the darkness seems far away. Yet just beyond the frame of the picture, the jungle—ageless, brooding—still lies patiently in wait.

hunting. Today, the Dayaks of Kalimantan substitute coconuts for real human heads, but expeditions in search of the genuine article were prevalent in some areas as recently as the 1960s.

An ebbing estuarine tide leaves behind it a careless scatter of beached boats, their hulls sunk deep in unappetising grey mud. Footprints define the tracks of their departing crews. When the waters return, the boatmen will be aboard their vessels once more, ready to resume the trade which keeps the settlements of Kalimantan in precarious contact with the outside world.

The earliest evidence of writing in Indonesia was found in Kalimantan, and relics of ancient Hindu-Buddhist kingdoms have been discovered here from time to time, but most contemporary settlements are of more recent origin. Kalimantan's highways are its rivers. Adventurers and traders in search of valuable minerals, spices and timber—Chinese, Buginese from Sulawesi, Malays and Europeans—were obliged to make their attempts on its interior by water, and their presence lent an unlikely cosmopolitan air to the towns which accreted around the coastal estuaries. These towns face outwards, towards the rivers, towards the sea: to the majority of their early inhabitants, the forest at their backs was an alien place infested with predators, disease, evil spirits and hostile tribes.

In the course of time some of the coastal centres evolved into sultanates, the two most noteworthy being Kutai and Banjarmasin (both of which, however, had their origin in pre-Islamic kingdoms). Their income depended on the interface between coastal trade and the riches of the interior—gold, diamonds and black pepper. The forests were a principle source of ironwood, a timber highly prized for its hardness, density and remarkable resistance to decay.

During the colonial period, Dutch and British traders competed to gain a foothold in the area, but it was not until the early part of the twentieth century that colonial authority was extended in any measure over Kalimantan.

By then it had become clear that the area was rich in oil. Modern Kalimantan is a storehouse of energy for Indonesia's growing industries. Oil and gas terminals dot the coast, while whole towns have been built on its promise and subsequent bounty. With development have come more immigrants: Buginese farmers from Sulawesi who open up coastal land for pepper farming, and Javanese transmigrants resettled in the area to escape the crushing shortage of rice-land in East Java. A monotony of tin roofs broken only by the occasional white dome of a mosque lends the landscape a more settled look than hitherto. Life is still not easy for a great number of these people. The climate is exceedingly harsh, the thin lateritic soils too poor to support the cultivation of crops.

By Indonesian standards, Kalimantan is a young region with bountiful (one might even say lucrative) prospects. But for the time being at least, in common with the rest of Borneo, those prospects remain largely undeveloped. It is the natural setting that dominates—much as it always has, the dark secret forbidding interior penetrated only by the rivers, along which the longhouses of the Dayak people cling with their backs to the forest.

One of the oldest mosques in Samarinda betrays Javanese ancestry in its foursquare plan and stepped, pyramidal roof. The minaret's antecedents are somewhat harder to trace—the architecture even seems to include touches of art deco, transmogrified by displacement in cultural and geographical space.

The great river town of Samarinda clings to the banks at the mouth of the Mahakam River in East Kalimantan. The main focus of activity here is nautical, for Samarinda is an important locus of the trade that runs up and down the river. Many of the town's inhabitants today are Buginese migrants from South Sulawesi, who brought with them their strong belief in Islam and a proud maritime tradition.

A plywood factory on a bend in the river. Indonesia has banned the export of raw logs in the hope that by creating secondary processing plants like this one, more income can be generated for the local people, and a higher added value engendered from the raw materials the forest provides. Preceding pages, looking down at this Kalimantan water village, one can understand how the great Sumatran kingdom of Srivijaya could have left behind so few traces of its existence—for Srivijaya, too, was a maritime community.

Even logs sometimes have to wait, though they seem no better at forming an orderly queue than many humans. Resembling randomly scattered matches thrown out of their box, these logs await their turn at the mill. Large-scale logging has been a major industry in Kalimantan for almost thirty years.

Straining against the powerful flow of the great Mahakam River, a carefully woven raft of logs awaits transport to the rivermouth. These great temporary constructions, frequently as long as tankers, travel great distances. They often move downriver at night, lit by oil lamps which warn passing traffic to stay clear.

The Mahakam River flows into the sea via a broad delta carpeted with mangrove swamps. Slowing as it reaches these flatter lands, the great river breaks up into myriad streams, winding lazily towards the sea. The ecology of these swamps is complex, with a host of different living creatures interacting to provide one another with sustenance. The forests of the interior are more variegated still; Borneo's wildlife riches are enormous, and many of its species are to be found nowhere else in the world.

The forest canopy. From the air, the height of these trees in the rainforest of East Kalimantan is misleading. It may be as much as a hundred metres from the treetops to the forest floor. Under the trees, the ground does not resemble the impenetrable tangle of vines and shrubs of popular myth. Too little sunlight filters through the thick canopy to ground level to support much more than a small amount of undergrowth.

Clearing the forest
and then making use
of the land is no easy
task. Once exposed,
the soil is easily
washed away and
loses its fertility rapidly.
Here the forest claws
back at the edges of
this settlement in a
bend of a small
tributary river.
Man's exploitation
of the resources of
Kalimantan, though
apparently so
destructive to the
environment, is still
very much at the
mercy of nature.

Man's search for oil sends him into the most forbidding of Indonesia's many environments. Here, a lone exploratory well stands in a clearing. Before sinking the well, a portion of forest has had to be cleared, and a dirt road cut. During the height of the worldwide oil crisis of the 1970s, petroleum exports accounted for eighty percent of Indonesia's earnings overseas. The country's economy today is far more diversified, though oil and petroleum-based products are still vitally important.

The majesty of the great Mahakam River, threading its way through the virtually untouched highland rainforest of East Kalimantan. Rounding the bend, a remote settlement hugs the banks for dear life, dependent on passing boatmen for all its links with the outside world.

POINTS EAST

Range after range
of tree-clad peaks
in central Irian Jaya
offer perhaps the
grandest landscape
in Indonesia,
preceding pages.
This massive province
lying at the eastern
end of the archipelago
has been barely
touched by man;
it remains one of the
world's last great
wilderness areas.
Left, Torajan villages
are traditionally built
on hilltops or ridges,
a legacy from the time
when wild bands of
headhunters roamed
the central highlands
of Sulawesi.

Indonesia's eastern islands mark the point at which Southeast Asia merges with the Pacific. Great land masses give way to island chains, and the uniformity of the rice-growing culture fades into a polyglot muddle of isolated societies. From island to island the landscape alters dramatically, straddling the transition between the equatorial tropics and Australasia's drier climatic zone. Westward, azure blue seas lap on the brilliant white shores framing small isles of emerald green. Further east, harsh dry seasons paint almost Mediterranean hues on scantily populated islands like Timor, where fresh water is scarce, vegetation struggles to survive, and irrigation is rudimentary or non-existent.

Some of these tiny, apparently impoverished eastern islands were once among the most valuable possessions of the old world. To early seafaring traders from Europe, spices from the Maluku islands were as precious as gold; the demand for them at home was nearly insatiable. Ternate, Tidore, Banda and Ambon were household words in sixteenth-century Europe, though these islands shared none of the regional importance of the mainland states of Java.

Europeans arriving in the Spice Islands found a semi-ordered state of anarchy. The sixteenth-century Portuguese chronicler Antonio Galvao reported from Maluku that 'every place was independent, with its own territory and boundaries...everyone (lived) at his own convenience. They were ruled by the voices of the eldest, of whom one was not better than the other...uproars, intrigues, dissensions and wars were continuously prevalent among them.'

Europeans were by no means the first visitors to the eastern archipelago. Malay and Chinese traders often passed this way, leaving behind indelible traces of their languages and cultures. The Portuguese in their turn brought Christianity, which took root on islands like Timor, Flores, and Ambon and has never been displaced. But the real struggle was for spices, not souls. Reading early accounts of frenetic trading, factional struggles, and attempts at colonization, it is hard to imagine so much activity taking place—and such importance being placed—on specks of land such as volcano-peaked Ternate and Tidore, where today a small aeroplane barely has room to land.

Eventually, the old Spice Islands became stable, peaceful outposts of Dutch hegemony. Christian Ambonese and Minahasans from North Sulawesi were prized as soldiers in the colonial army. Yet despite the appearance of subjugation, the islanders continued to live as before, sustained by abundant food and the strong communal bonds which are still apparent today.

Further south, the island chain of Nusa Tenggara experienced almost no contact with the modern world until the

The production of salt is one means of making low-lying coastal areas in Java, Sulawesi and Sumba productive: sea water floods large pans, evaporates, and the resulting residue is processed to yield salt. These pans are in Sulawesi.

A peculiar feature of these Sumbanese villages is the apparent willingness of the villagers to live side by side with their dead ancestors. The huge slab-like stone tombs are located close to the peak-roofed clan houses, perhaps as a reminder of how close death once was to these people, in the days when fighting was endemic and subsistence in the arid climate of Sumba was no certainty at all.

early twentieth century. The Dutch fitfully colonized the islands of Sumba, Flores and Timor towards the end of their rule, and East Timor continued as a forgotten relic of the long-departed Portuguese empire until the mid-1970s. Under Indonesian administration, these islands have remained gentle backwaters.

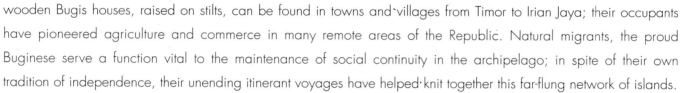

Snowcapped Puncak Jaya, marooned amid the impenetrable forests of Irian Jaya's interior, was a secret well hidden from Western eyes—indeed, from all human eyes, barring those of a few Neolithic tribesmen—until the advent of the aeroplane.

Sulawesi has always claimed pre-eminence among the eastern islands. The seafaring Buginese, originally from the city of Makasar, now inhabit much of the east. Distinctive, peak-roofed wooden Bugis houses, raised on stilts, can be found in towns and villages from Timor to Irian Jaya; their occupants have pioneered agriculture and commerce in many remote areas of the Republic. Natural migrants, the proud Buginese serve a function vital to the maintenance of social continuity in the archipelago; in spite of their own tradition of independence, their unending itinerant voyages have helped knit together this far-flung network of islands.

Modern Sulawesi sees itself as a gateway to the east. Makasar (now Ujung Pandang) has shrugged off three hundred years of colonial somnolence to become an important centre of trade between eastern and western Indonesia. With almost a million souls, one of the best universities outside Java, and an impressive network of sea and air connections, Ujung Pandang is perhaps one of the fastest growing centres in the Western Pacific.

The strength of Bugis culture and its aggressive history have not rendered Sulawesi wholly Buginese. Tucked away in the highlands above Ujung Pandang lies the homeland of the Toraja, a people whose roots may be traced back to tribal migrations from Central Asia. Practicing their ancient, animistic burial rites (and gaining in the process a handsome income from tourism), the Toraja symbolize the prodigal ethnic variety of this region. Their distinctively carved houses, with rakishly angled thatched roofs, are further evidence of the lasting diversity of Indonesia.

Irian Jaya consists of the western half of the island of New Guinea, so-called because early explorers mistook its dark-skinned Melanesian inhabitants for Africans. It is a magnificent landscape, ranging from the snow-capped Jayawijaya mountains to the arid Merauke coastal lands dominated by termite hills and gum trees. Its population is scattered among remote valleys which till very recently had no contact with one another, much less the outside world.

Large-scale settlement is difficult here; the land and climate are unsuitable to rice cultivation. Schools and hospitals are difficult to organize where population densities drop as low as two people per square kilometre. Commerce is hard to foster in a traditional barter economy. Yet some Buginese and Javanese do come, to settle around the capital, Jayapura, and eke out an existence in one of the most forbidding landscapes of the archipelago.

Manado, the capital of North Sulawesi, is the cultural home of the Minahasan people. This mainly Christian group were thoroughly colonized by the Dutch, whose influence is enduring, as the church suggests. Before the Dutch came the Spanish and the Portuguese, who first arrived in North Sulawesi during the sixteenth century. They left many traces of their culture and language, which still pervade the region.

The aroma from these warehouses lining the quayside offers a reminder that the city of Manado was born and grew rich of the spice trade. Cloves and coconuts remain the area's primary exports. Strolling by the waterside, one invariably encounters pungent sacks of dried cloves and nutmeg being prepared for loading.

Fort Rotterdam
stands as a reminder
of the long and eventful
Dutch involvement in
Makasar and the island
of Celebes, which
began in the early
seventeenth century
with attempts to
monopolize the spice
trade. In 1667, a final
attempt succeeded.
With its steep Dutch
gables and well-
preserved form,
the fort is the best
entirely surviving
example of Dutch
imperial architecture
in Sulawesi.

The quayside at the ancient port of Makasar—now called Ujung Pandang. The city's Buginese sailors have been plying the seas of the region for centuries in ships not very different from these modern workhorses. Their considerable girth and curved lines allow these sea-going prahus to carry considerable tonnages without drawing too much water, an important consideration since the shallow waters of the archipelago are liberally endowed with shoals, sandbars, submerged reefs and other obstacles.

A hot, sulphurous lake steams within this classically-shaped crater in North Sulawesi. The greenery covering its outer slopes lends a benign look to the landscape, but the appearance of enduring calm is decptive. The northern 'tail' of Sulawesi lies near the junction of no less than four great tectonic plates, shifting restlessly against one another as they float on the earth's molten mantle. Earthquakes and eruptions are commonplace occurrences here. Quiescent but restless, the volcano presides over a landscape that draws fertility from its lava-clad slopes, but which is always at the mercy of its moods. Indonesia's volcanoes lend its landscapes a sense of mutability; in the archipelago, it is as if the Act of Creation had not yet ended.

Entering the beautiful
mountains and valleys
of Torajaland means
leaving the present
behind and being
engulfed by a small
world of unchanging
customs and beliefs.
These central highlands
of South Sulawesi
remained more or less
cut off from the outside
world until the early
part of this century.
Yet despite the
encroachment of
outside influences since
then, the Toraja people
retain a strong sense
of their own identity,
high up above the
plains of Makasar.

Sulawesi boasts a landscape diversified by irrigated plains, lush rainforests, deep valleys and steep mountains. Rice is the main crop grown on the plains, while maize and sago are cultivated on higher terrain.

The cultivated coastal plains, seen from above, form a gigantic complex patchwork and contrast with the rugged and unexplored parts of inland Sulawesi.

The ordered contours of these terraced ricefields in South Sulawesi suggest a natural form, perhaps a volcanic flow of some sort, or the manner in which cooling wax pools at the foot of a burning candle. In fact, it illustrates vividly the farmer's skill at exploiting the natural morphology of the land, ensuring that each field will receive a carefully-measured sufficiency of water.

Water, the vital sustenance of the padi rice ecology. The rains swell the rivers and flood the fields, which retain their water because a hard pan of alluvial soil, carefully constructed and maintained, underlies each of them.

Rice is one of the most water-intensive crops of all, and the devices employed in the management of this vital resource are among the most visible components of the agricultural landscape of Sulawesi.

The plains of South Sulawesi are the granaries of eastern Indonesia, the easternmost outpost of rice cultivation in the region. The flooded fields draw on a complex network of irrigation canals which must be managed and maintained with care. The reward, provided all goes well, is reaped in a riot of colour at harvest time.

The kampong or village is the basic unit of Indonesian society. Its physical form expresses communal endeavour and collective security, bound by faith and hemmed in with fields tended by its people. Anthropologists link this phenomenon to the necessities of life in a predominantly agricultural society, and certainly the pattern is remarkably similar in all the rice-growing societies of Indonesia, on Java, Bali, Sulawesi and elsewhere in the archipelago.

Man against
nature. Forests
in places like Central
Sulawesi are hard to
clear, and once
cultivated the land
quickly loses its fertility,
the thin, erosion-prone
soil with its vital
nutrients washed
away by periodic
heavy rains. The
torrent that flows by
this clearing bears
witness to the problems
of soil erosion.

This curving bay in an island off the coast of Sulawesi shelters a small fishing community whose main lifeline to civilization is a periodic visit from an itinerant steamer—a situation which has endured since the days when Conrad wrote his story The End of the Tether, which tells of the voyages of just such a ship. Anchored in deep water at the very edge of the coral shelf that fringes the bay, the vessel discharges mail, news from the world outside, and all the necessaries of life which the island's own ecology cannot provide.

Combing the sea's edge. The layout of this coastal village appears to be that of a vast net or strainer designed to capture all it can of the ocean's wealth. Often at high tide, the houses of such a settlement are completely isolated by the sea, and neighbours visit one another or the mainland by boat.

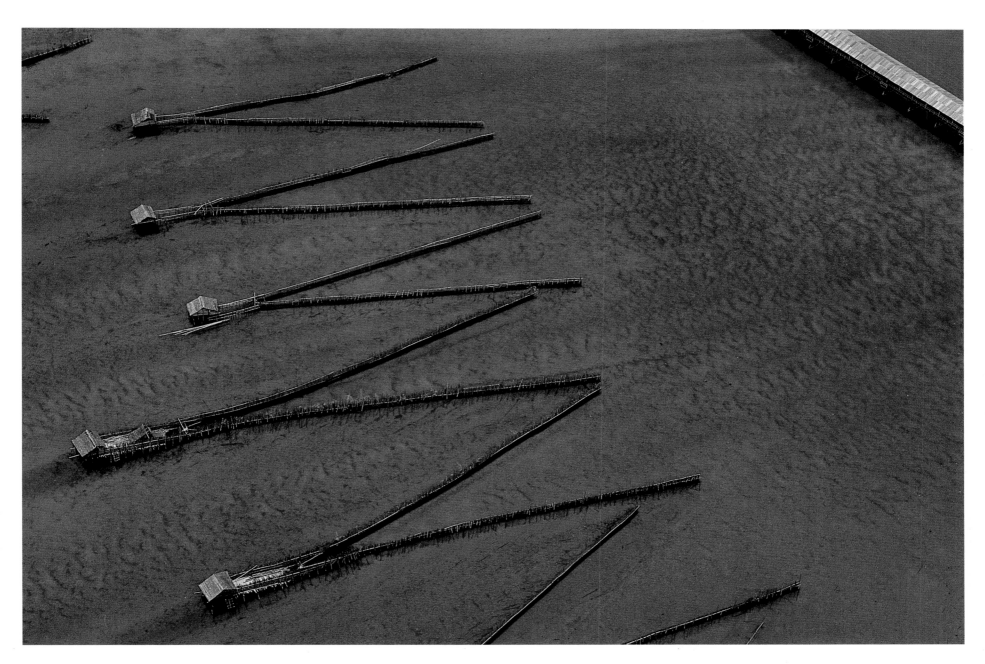

Fishtraps are not confined to the shallow coastal waters of the Java Sea. These Y-shaped fishtraps in Lake Posso, Central Sulawesi, are open to the prevailing current which drives fish along the netted alleys, supported by wooden stakes driven into the soft mud, and into large nets slung beneath the thatched bamboo platforms.

The sea around Sulawesi is renowned for its coral formations, and the northern and central coastal regions of the island offer some of the best diving to be enjoyed anywhere in the archipelago. The island of Togian, rising from the water at the geometric centre of the 200-km-wide bay formed by the curving tail of Sulawesi, is surrounded by a host of tiny coral islets which make up Kepuluan Togian, or the Togian Group.

Most of the islets, like the one above, are preserves of uninhabited wilderness, remote from Indonesia's centres of population. It will be many years before they are carved up to make way for tourism. They remain best appreciated from the air: a natural mosaic composed of the two most important Indonesian elements: land and water.

A coastal road meanders along a wooded hillside on the Sulawesi coast, seeming to follow the curve of the offshore coral shelf. Over the shelf the water is less than a metre, sometimes only a few centimetres deep, but beyond it the sea is navigable by a sizeable ship. The sea around these islands is generally shallow, but a few hundred kilometres to the northeast the ocean floor plunges steeply downward to form the Mindanao Trench, where depths reach 9,000 metres or even more.

Clinging to its rocky islet like a cluster of barnacles to the side of a clamshell, this tiny fishing village off the coast of Sulawesi could be, depending on the observer's viewpoint, either a lost paradise or an exile's purgatory.

Once upon a time, Manado was an elegant, and sleepy, colonial market town. Modern development and commerce have changed its face considerably: so much so that the principal city of North Sulawesi is now beginning to have to cope with the unlovely problems of urban sprawl, right. However, one does not have to travel far from the city to encounter small communities like this one, above, on the island of Bunaken, where the pace of life is still as leisurely as ever, and the abundant sunshine is still something to bask in rather than avoid.

Gentle beasts of burden wallow in a dwindling Sumbawa stream. This remote eastern island is renowned for its livestock, though from the colour of the landscape, there seems scarcely enough water here to support life.

West Nusa Tenggara's arid landscapes, here on the island of Sumbawa, evoke images of the Central Asian steppes: flat, parched expanses of country grazed by cattle and horses. In spite of the scarcity of water, however, Sumbawa's major exports are all agricultural: rice, peanuts, beans and cattle.

Life is not easy for the Sumbawan farmer. Water conservation technology is often primitive, and modern methods sometimes prove inappropriate to the landscape and culture. Still, things are better than they once were: the traditional Sumbawan diet, fish and sago roots, has given way to a rather more diverse menu.

The traditional cultures of Eastern Indonesia offer a fascinating diversity of artifacts, from ritual objects to some of the world's most beautiful textiles. The shapes and forms of these artifacts are often unique to a particular culture; witness this Sumbawan village, with its thatch-roofed houses thrusting up from among the flat stone tombs of the villagers' forbears.

Violent eruptions and lava flows sculpted the hills and valleys around Mount Tambora in Sumbawa, creating natural slopes and terraces that the local inhabitants have transformed into terraced ricefields. The people of Sumbawa are among the most devout of Indonesia's Muslims, and the ambition of every farmer is a series of harvests abundant enough to enable him to make the long-desired pilgrimage to Mecca. Many realize that ambition; eastern Sumbawa boasts more hajis per capita than any other part of Indonesia.

In 1815 Tambora was the site of the world's greatest volcanic explosion. Its force was of thermo-nuclear proportions; more than a hundred cubic kilometres of debris were ejected into the air. The eruption affected the climate of the entire globe; debris in the upper atmosphere blotted out sunlight and lowered temperatures throughout the following year. A small cinder cone on the flank of Mount Tambora hints at the power of the volcano.

These fishing boats take to the sea at nightfall. Petrol lamps laid along the bamboo structures around the boats attract schools of fish. The waters east off Indonesia are still rich, though Indonesians now share the bounty with international fishing fleets.

Black sand of volcanic origin gives the sea a forbidding hue, but these fishermen, preparing their boats for another foray, seem unconcerned.

There seems little this offshore fishing community near Sumbawa, left, could ask for: it already possesses tranquillity, calm and a plentiful source of food. The ocean is rich in fish, and the methods used to trap them are both ancient and effective. Much of eastern Indonesia remains preserved in anachronistic stasis, perhaps because the old ways of life remain the most comfortable. Above, dust upon the sea: the tiny islets which make up so much of the eastern archipelago.

High above the
agricultural landscape
of Sumbawa, the
photographer captures
the timeless geometries
of community and
cultivation. The island
is nearly twice the size
of Bali, yet supports

only 800,000 people;
this population has
grown from a figure of
approximately zero
after the great eruption
of 1815. It is a far cry
from the congestion
of Java, some 500km
to the east.

Salt pans glitter in the harsh Sumbawan sunlight. The climate of the island, so inimical to most other forms of cultivation, is ideal for this most difficult and unrewarding of all methods of human subsistence.

The coloured lakes of Keli Mutu in central Flores, sulphurous reminders of the island's volcanic character. Flores is home to some of Indonesia's most active volcanoes, having the largest number outside Java. The three lakes occupying the Keli Mutu crater complex change their colours over time, suggesting a vast natural inkpot. According to local legend, the crater lakes are inhabited by the souls of the departed, and it is their moods and activities which cause the changes of colour; it is a more succint explanation than many of the scientific ones which have been advanced for the phenomenon.

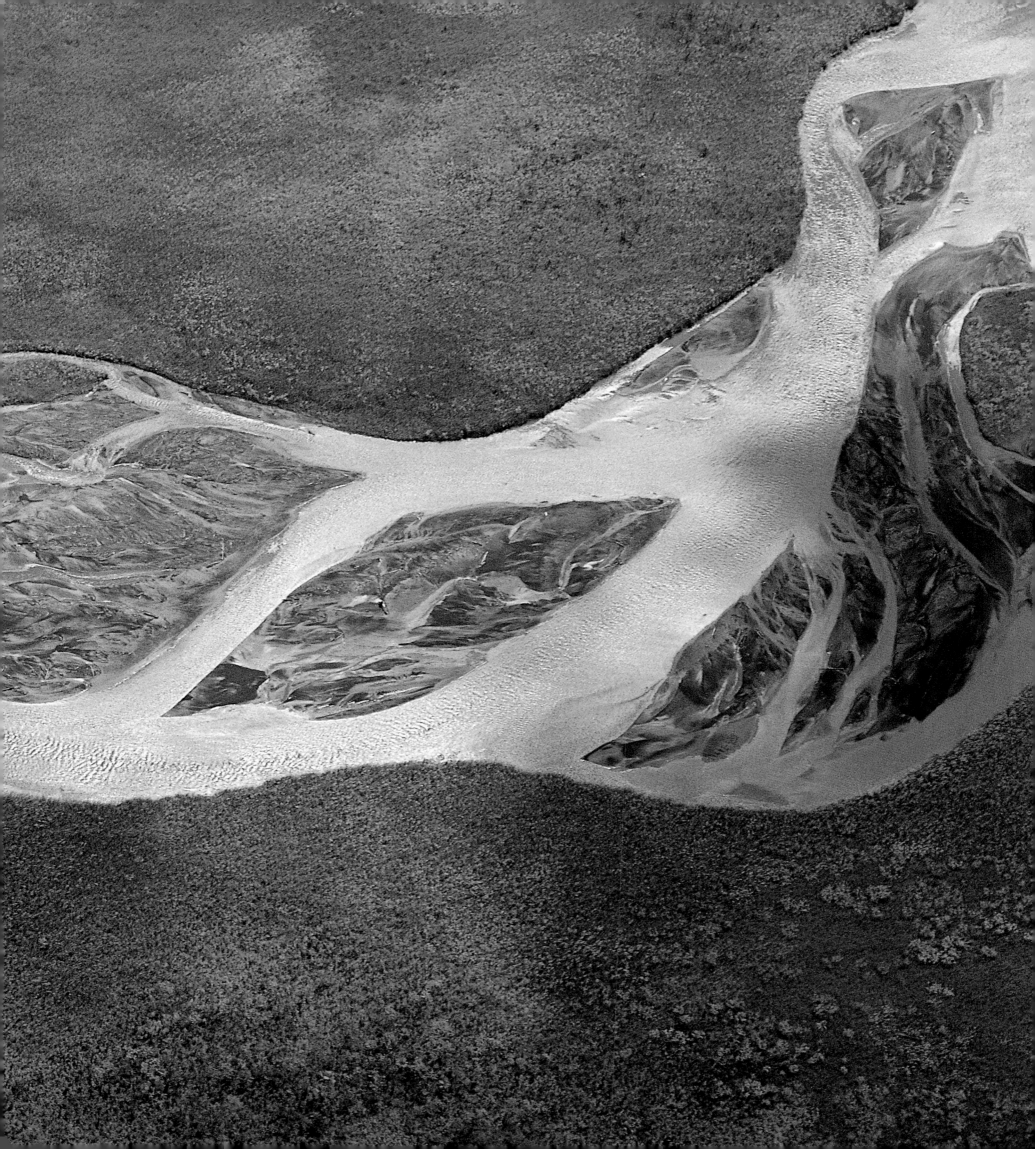

Natural sinews
of water stretch across
a highland valley in
Irian Jaya, preceding
pages. Here nature
often appears
forbidding, magnified
and overpowering,
as upon the soil of
an unexplored planet.
The Dani people of
Irian Jaya build villages
which comprise
a network of self-
contained compounds,
left, each with its own
gardens and pigsty.
The pig is a valued
possession, the number
owned being an
indicator of status.
Much has changed
in the Baliem valley
since it was discovered,
though traditional
patterns of settlement
seem little disturbed.

Like an ancient map, irrigation channels built with stone tools and sharpened sticks trace a crude path of liquid nourishment. The Dani farmers in Irian Jaya's Baliem valley are skilled cultivators, and are renowned for their gardens. When the valley was first discovered in 1938, the explorer Richard Archbold thought he was looking at vegetable plots from Central Europe.

Cultivation in the valleys; habitation on the ridge-tops. The pattern is as old as man's history of settlement. Here in Irian Jaya's lush intermontaine valleys, hardly any aspect of village life has changed for thousands of years, in what is possibly the last place on earth where the earliest patterns of collective human society are still to be found.

The indigenous peoples of Irian Jaya still live largely as they have done since prehistoric times. The province's interior was terra incognita, a blank space on the map, until very recently. Large tracts of Irian Jaya remain unexplored today, some four hundred years after it was first discovered for the West by spice traders whose oriental wanderings had taken them beyond the waters they knew. The first expeditions to the interior were only mounted at the beginning of the present century.

A deep blue fresh-water lake rimmed with forest, in Irian Jaya. The province's geography is extremely variable, with several different ecosystems coexisting in areas very close to one another: among them are swampland, jungle and soaring mountain ranges. Few of them are as inviting as this peaceful, isolated spot.

Flat land is scarce in Irian Jaya. Here a hem of tin roofs and stilted dwellings makes good use of the available space along the shores of Lake Santani. Not far inland the dangers of the interior bring settlement to a virtual halt. Water is scarce, land clearance difficult and roads non-existent more than 50km outside the capital, Jayapura.

An awe-inspiring expanse of rolling jungle threatens to engulf Irian Jaya's largest settlement, Jayapura. The town lies on the north coast, close to the border with Papua New Guinea. Yet the heart of this provincial capital, with its busy markets, shops and foodstalls, beats scarcely slower than any other Indonesian town's. Near the harbour, a large diesel generator thumps away day and night to keep the city lit. Following pages: snowcapped Jaya Peak, rising nearly 5,000 metres above sea level in Irian Jaya's central mountain massif, is the highest mountain in the world east of the Himalayas, high enough for its upper slopes to be blanketed in snow in spite of its location barely four degrees below the Equator.

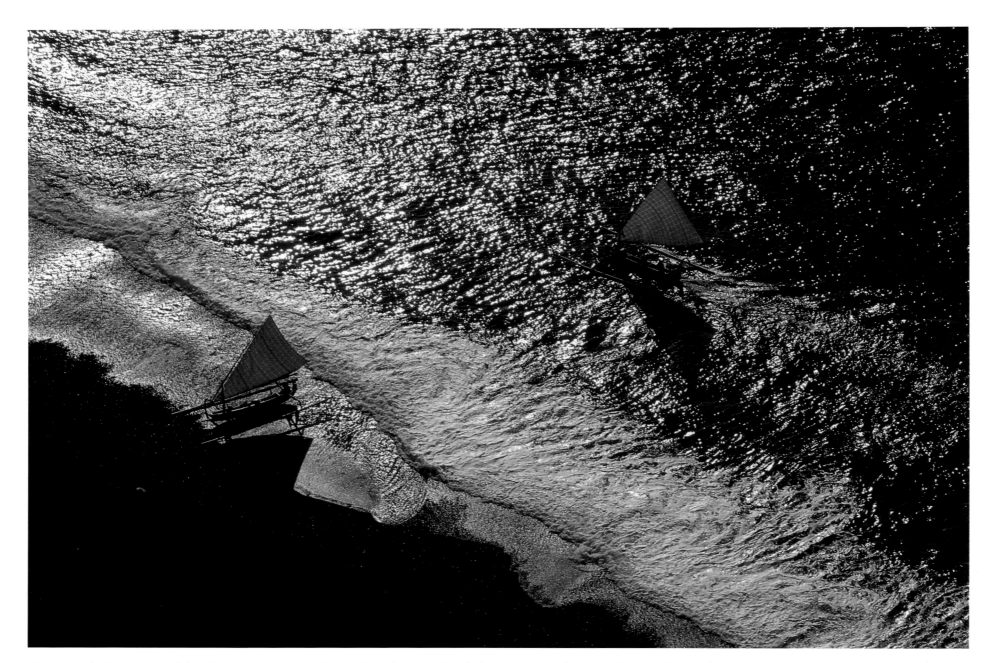

The publishers would like to express their thanks to the following: Gatari Air Service/Humpuss Group and the Mission Aviation Fellowship for aircraft and pilots; the Indonesian Armed Forces and in particular the Armed Forces Survey and Mapping Center; Mr. Victor Siburian and Mrs. Halida Hatta Jusuf of Caltex; the staff at Gatari Air Service, at the office of Prof. Habibie, at Hilton International Jakarta and at P.T. Sempati Air; the staff at the office of Pak Joop Ave and Pak Joop himself, without whose assistance this project would never have been realized. We should also like to acknowledge generous contributions by the sponsors of the Over Indonesia project: BPP Teknologi (The Agency for the Assessment and Application of Technology), Caltex, Freeport Indonesia Incorporated, Gatari Air Service/Humpuss Group, Hilton International Jakarta, P.T. Sempati Air and Total Indonesia.